Angry
Kids
Frustrated
Parents

Also from the Boys Town Press

For Parents
Common Sense Parenting® (book and audiobook)
Common Sense Parenting® Learn-at-Home Video Kit
Common Sense Parenting® of Toddlers and Preschoolers
Practical Tools for Foster Parents
Parenting After September 11, 2001
Parenting to Build Character in Your Teen
Boys Town Videos for Parents Series
Sign with Me (video sign language instruction)
La Crianza Práctica de los Hijos

For Youth
Boundaries: A Guide for Teens
Getting Along with Others
A Good Friend: How to Make One, How to Be One
Who's in the Mirror? Finding the Real Me
What's Right for Me? Making Good Choices in Relationships

For Youth Care and Education Professionals
Teaching Social Skills to Youth
Unmasking Sexual Con Games:
   Helping Teens Identify Good and Bad Relationships
Treating Youth with DSM-IV Disorders
The Well-Managed Classroom
Dangerous Kids
Building Skills in High-Risk Families
Skills for Families, Skills for Life
Working with Aggressive Youth
Caring for Youth in Shelters

**For a Boys Town Press catalog, call 1-800-282-6657 or
visit our website at www.girlsandboystown.org/btpress.**

Angry
Kids
Frustrated
Parents

Practical Ways to Prevent and Reduce Aggression in Your Children

Terry L. Hyland
Jerry Davis, Ph.D.

BOYS
TOWN
PRESS

BOYS TOWN, NEBRASKA

Angry Kids, Frustrated Parents

Published by the Boys Town Press
Father Flanagan's Boys' Home
Boys Town, Nebraska 68010

Publisher's Cataloging-in-Publication
(Provided by Quality Books, Inc.)

Hyland, Terry L.
    Angry kids, frustrated parents : practical ways to prevent and reduce aggression in your children / Terry L. Hyland, Jerry Davis. -- 1st ed.
    p. cm.
    Includes index.
    ISBN: 1-889322-28-8

    1. Child rearing. 2. Child psychology.
3. Aggressiveness (Psychology) in adolescence.
4. Aggressiveness (Psychology) in children. I. Davis, Jerry, 1947- II. Father Flanagan's Boys' Home. III. Title.

HQ773.H75 1999   649'.64
           QBI99-399

10   9   8   7   6   5   4   3

Acknowledgments

This book would not have been possible without the dedicated and ongoing efforts of many people. We would like to thank the following Boys Town administrators and staff for their contributions to this project: Father Val J. Peter, Executive Director; Jack Nelson, Senior Training Specialist; Ron Herron, Director of the Writing Division; and Dr. Robert Larzelere, Director of Residential Research.

A special thanks goes to Dr. Patrick Friman, Director of Specialized Clinical Services and Research at Boys Town, for allowing us to use selected portions of his research study in this book. Dr. Friman's help and cooperation is greatly appreciated.

The Boys Town Press is the publishing division of Girls and Boys Town, the original Father Flanagan's Boys' Home.

Kids with any kind of problem can call the Girls and Boys Town National Hotline anytime at 1-800-448-3000.

Table of Contents

Introduction

Phillip has a reputation as a bad kid. In his neighborhood, he constantly beats up on the smaller kids, throws rocks at people's houses, and curses when things don't go his way. He's also been caught slashing car tires. At school, he's been in trouble for stealing from other students and fighting. Lately, Phillip has been hitting and kicking his younger brother and sister, and both of them are afraid to be around him.

Phillip usually denies doing anything wrong when he gets caught. But as soon as he sees there's no way to avoid being punished, he'll say he's sorry and promise to be good. A few days will pass with no problems. Then the aggressive behaviors start again. This has been going on for six months.

1

Phillip is 15 years old. What would you do if he was your son?

Every parent has seen his or her child hit, push, yell at, take something from, pick on, or fight with another child. It's the way children – especially young children – get what they want before they learn more positive ways of getting along with others. In most families, these behaviors result in some kind of negative consequences for the child. Over time, the child begins to understand that hurting others is not the way to solve problems or settle differences. Even more importantly, the child learns positive ways to get his or her needs met. These are the skills a child must have in order to find success in adolescence and adulthood.

But what happens when a child displays a pattern of hurtful, destructive behavior? Can most parents identify such activity as the start of a problem that, if left unchecked, could lead to more serious negative behavior? Can most parents distinguish between the normal growing-up behaviors mentioned earlier and behaviors that could be signaling the onset of aggression in a child?

Aggression among youth is a growing problem in our society. At its lowest level, it can include behaviors like not following instructions, whining, crying, and teasing. At its most extreme, it can involve assault, rape, robbery, and murder.

How do children move from child-like innocence to single-minded aggression? And how can these children "unlearn" the aggressive behaviors they have come to depend on? There are no easy answers to these questions, which makes the task of figuring out how to deal with aggression even more difficult.

As a parent, you are responsible for helping your children choose the right path as they grow in society. That path can sometimes be rocky, with challenges and obstacles that must be overcome. That's where Boys Town can help. This book has two goals: 1) to help parents recognize aggressive behavior in their children and act before it becomes a problem, and 2) to show parents how they can teach their children to stop using negative aggressive behaviors and learn new positive behaviors.

Aggression is a complex issue. Like any behavior problem, it must be identified as a problem before the process of change can begin. This is not always easy. The common thinking is that children use aggression only when they are angry; the image most parents have of an aggressive child is one who physically lashes out at others when he or she is mad. But while anger frequently is involved, kids can turn to aggression for other reasons. Some aggressive kids are motivated by factors like jealousy, spite, or the need for control, and actually plan out their attacks on others. Others use subtle aggressive behaviors that adults who don't know what to look for might miss or ignore. Still other kids – especially bullies – pick on or torment others for fun or "kicks."

When it comes to treating or dealing with aggression, every child is different, and what works with one boy or girl might not work with another. There are no magic "cures." That doesn't mean there isn't hope. In its more than 80 years of working with troubled children, Boys Town has developed proven, effective treatment strategies that have helped youth with many kinds of behavior and emotional problems, including aggression. Combined with a parent's love, these strategies can reduce aggressive behaviors and teach children that success is achieved through treating others with respect, kindness, and compassion.

Parents are the architects of their children's future. Whether you want to prevent problems with aggression or are looking for a way to stop your child's aggressive behavior, we hope this book can be a useful, informative, and insightful blueprint for success.

Aggressive Kids

CHAPTER 1

What Is Aggression?

B efore we can talk about the best ways to prevent
or correct aggression in children, we have to
know what aggression is. This is important because
as you look at how your children behave, you must
determine whether negative behaviors directed at
others are merely part of the growing-up process or
are part of a pattern that is defining the type of person your child is becoming. In other words, are these
behaviors occurring once in a while, in situations
where you might expect children to squabble or
argue (two kids want to play with the same toy), or
does the child resort to them every time he or she
wants something or has to solve a problem?

For our purposes, we use this definition of
aggression: *Standing up for one's self in dishonest
and inappropriate ways that violate the rights of*

7

another person.[1] This is a good definition because it goes to the heart of the worst aspect of aggression – hurting others. This covers many behaviors: arguing, fighting, taking something from someone, calling others names, pushing and shoving, hitting, kicking, showing disrespect for others, making fun of others, refusing to follow instructions, and ignoring authority figures. At its most tragic extreme, it also includes acts like fatal school shootings or gang murders that shock and frighten people across the country.

This chapter and the next two offer information that is essential for parents who want to learn new ways of preventing or dealing with aggression in their children. This chapter and Chapter 2 will focus on defining what aggression is and what it is not. Chapter 3 will describe the two main types of aggression – planned and reactive – and discuss bullying.

What Aggression Is

Aggression is a complex issue. There is a difference between an aggressive child and a child who sometimes uses aggressive behaviors. An aggressive child has learned to rely on force, intimidation, or disobedience as ways to control people or situations. A child who sometimes uses aggressive behaviors either has not learned or doesn't always remember to use positive skills for solving problems. Neither situation is good, and both cry out for skillful teaching by parents. But it is much more difficult to "remove" aggression after it's become the major part of a child's personality than it is to help a youngster change aggressive behaviors that occur only occasionally.

Parents must consider a number of factors when trying to make this distinction:

- How often are aggressive behaviors occurring?
- How severe are the behaviors?
- Do the behaviors get worse when the child doesn't get his or her way?
- Does minor misbehavior seem to be giving way to more violent, hurtful behaviors?
- Are others afraid of the child?

The earlier parents see that children are turning to aggression, the more likely they are to change this pattern of behavior and teach their children other ways to settle differences or get what they want.

Children and adolescents display aggression in many different ways. At the extreme end, they commit violent acts like robbery, rape, and murder. While this type of behavior seems to be on the rise among youth, the percentage of young people who are involved in such serious criminal activity is relatively small. Therefore, it's safe to assume that most parents are familiar with more subtle forms of aggressive behavior from their children. For example, a daughter might whine and complain each time her parents ask her to clean up her messy room; this is her way of getting out of the chore. Or a son might glare at his mom when she tells him he can't have the new bicycle he sees in the store; this might be his way of trying to intimidate her into buying the bike.

These types of "minor" aggressive behaviors are harder to detect than more serious behaviors and are sometimes ignored or overlooked. In fact, some parents might not even consider behaviors like whining, glaring, ignoring, crying, and many others to be signs of aggression. But they are. The danger here is that if parents don't recognize this and don't intervene to reduce or stop such behaviors, children may believe that it's okay to continue to use them. Over time, these children may turn to more serious aggressive behaviors to get what they want.

Five Levels of Aggression

Let's take a look at the different levels of aggression and some examples of each one. Boys Town developed this system as a way to put behaviors in categories, starting with those that are minor or subtle and ending with those that are most serious or harmful. This is a good guide for identifying and evaluating negative behaviors, no matter how subtle they may be.

Level 1 - Noncompliance and/or Making Threatening Statements or Gestures

A youngster regularly responds to instructions with subtle forms of aggression or threatens other people.

Examples (noncompliance):

- Repeatedly refusing to do what a parent, teacher, or other authority figure asks
- Whining and crying
- Making sarcastic remarks
- Criticizing
- Teasing

Examples (threats):

- Using demanding statements (e.g., "Make me something to eat!")
- Repeating a behavior in order to annoy others (e.g., singing loudly or pounding a fist on a table)
- Staring and glaring
- Clenching a fist or both fists
- Cursing and yelling
- Ultimatums (e.g., "If you don't take me to the movie, I'm gonna break your lamp!")
- Invading someone's personal space
- Physically aggressive posturing (e.g., standing over a person in a threatening manner)

Level 2 - Causing Property Damage

A youngster frequently damages property.
Examples:

- Throwing objects
- Punching or kicking objects (e.g., punching or kicking a hole through a wall)
- Vandalism
- Stealing
- Setting fires

Level 3 - Harming Animals

A youngster frequently is cruel to animals or harms them.
Examples:

- Teasing an animal
- Throwing an object at an animal
- Hitting or kicking an animal
- Intentionally hurting an animal in any other way

Level 4 - Physically Harming Others or Self

A youngster consistently hurts others or himself or herself, but doesn't cause long-lasting or permanent physical or psychological damage.

Examples:

- Poking a finger into someone's chest
- Pushing or shoving
- Throwing or kicking objects at others
- Wrestling
- Punching
- Fighting
- Attempting to hurt self (e.g., cutting one's skin)

Level 5 - Using Violence

A youngster physically hurts others, himself or herself, or animals in ways that cause long-lasting or permanent physical or psychological damage.

Examples:

- Stalking
- Bomb threats
- Terrorism
- Intentionally torturing or killing an animal
- Aggravated assault
- Rape
- Suicide
- Murder

We said earlier that aggression is a complex issue. That is especially true when we are trying to determine how and why children move from one level to another. Some children and adolescents who reach Level 5 (using violence) have moved from one behavior to the next within a level, and then from one level to the next. There are kids, however, who might suddenly move from Level 1 behaviors like noncompliance and making threats to a Level 5 act like assault or murder. With these kids, there sometimes are few or no warning signs that they are about to commit a highly aggressive or violent act.

Generally speaking, kids who knowingly use aggression move through the levels in a more logical, predictable way. It is very important to remember that every child is different and each child's situation is unique. So how slowly or quickly a youth moves from one level to the next if there is no effort to stop the aggressive behaviors would depend on what's happening in that child's life.

The five levels are simply guidelines, a tool that can help parents and other caregivers assess the seriousness of a youth's aggression problem and determine what course of action to take. The levels should not be used to label youngsters or indicate that they are beyond help.

At this point, you might be saying: "Yes, my child whines once in a while. He even yells at me or hits me when he doesn't get his way. But that doesn't mean he's going to grow up to be a robber or a murderer. He's just being a kid."

And you're right; your child probably isn't going to be that kind of person. What we are suggesting is that aggression usually has its beginnings in childhood and parents must know the behaviors that signal a problem. Only then can you decide how to correct those behaviors. (We will discuss how to do that later in this book.) Remember that aggression usually involves a consistent pattern of aggressive behaviors, whether they are minor or serious. If these behaviors are allowed to continue, and worsen, a child can come to depend on them to get his or her way through adolescence into adulthood. The stage is then set for a life that can be full of hardship and pain for that person and others.

[1] Lange, A.J., & Jakubowski, P. (1976). **Responsible assertive behavior: Cognitive/behavioral procedures for trainers.** Champaign, IL: Research Press.

CHAPTER 2

Anger, Assertiveness, or Aggression?

The five levels are a good way to illustrate what aggression is and the wide range of behaviors that can be part of it. However, it is equally important for parents to know that there are certain behaviors that may appear to be aggressive, but in reality are not. Anger and assertiveness fall into this category.

When parents know what aggression is not, it is easier for them to tell the difference between appropriate behavior that should be praised and reinforced, and harmful behavior that should be corrected. For example, a youth who gets what she wants by being outspoken and confident might be criticized for being aggressive when, in fact, she is only showing some independence. If she is standing up for herself without violating someone's rights, she's not being aggressive. The line between aggressive and acceptable behaviors can sometimes be unclear, making it difficult for parents to decide what to do. The next section will look at how anger and assertiveness are sometimes mistaken for aggression and the factors that determine when they cross over into aggression. We also will briefly discuss the rare instances when aggression may be a necessary and appropriate response.

Aggression and Anger

After dinner, Jose's mom asked him to do the dishes. Jose, 10, got mad. He stood in the kitchen with his arms folded and complained that he always gets stuck with all the hard work. Mom listened to Jose, then told him to get busy. Knowing his mom wouldn't give in, Jose filled the sink and went to work.

Shana wants to go to a party this weekend with her friends. But her grandmother is visiting from out of town and the family has planned a picnic on the same day as the party. When her dad tells her she won't be able to go out with her friends, Shana starts yelling and swearing. Dad responds by grounding Shana for a week.

This really sets her off. She storms to her room, slams the door, and starts trashing the place. Her dad comes in and tries to stop her. Then Shana rushes outside and heads for a friend's house across the street as her dad yells for her to get back in the house. When she ignores him, he sits down and wonders why this happens whenever he has to tell his daughter she can't do something.

Anger is a feeling that all youngsters commonly experience during childhood and adolescence. Anger can be justified or unjustified. A child might feel justified anger in a situation where she learns that a friend lied to her or she discovers that someone stole her bicycle. An example of unjustified anger would be a situation where a child gets angry because his mom tells him he can't have a piece of cake before dinner.

In the examples with Jose and Shana, neither child was justified in getting angry. However, there was a difference in how they reacted and behaved when they got mad. Jose got angry about having to do the dishes. But he didn't do much more than stand in the kitchen and complain. His angry feelings didn't lead to overtly aggressive behaviors, and they disappeared quickly. Jose probably felt like he made his point, even though he knew he wasn't going to get out of doing the dishes.

Shana's anger, on the other hand, led to a series of aggressive behaviors that resulted in a fight between her and her dad. Her way of reacting to situations when she gets mad is to strike out in destructive and harmful ways. This results in many negative consequences, like getting grounded. Even worse is the damage these incidents cause to the relationship between Shana and her parents.

Whether anger is justified or not, youngsters must learn how to control their feelings and the behaviors they use to express them. One way parents can help their kids do this is by teaching them not to get angry when they don't get what they want or when things don't go their way. When kids learn that they can control negative thoughts and feelings, they will be better able to control negative behaviors. (This will be discussed in more detail later.)

While anger often triggers aggressive behavior in children, and can be a signal that such behavior is going to occur, parents must be able to tell the difference between the two. Aggression doesn't happen only when a child is angry, and an angry child doesn't necessarily equal an aggressive child.

Aggression and Assertiveness

Sixteen-year-old Marcia really wanted to win her high school science fair. She especially wanted to beat Annie, a classmate whom Marcia doesn't like.

The science fair rules forbid parents from helping students with their projects; students are supposed to do all the work themselves. But Marcia never showed the rules to her parents and convinced her dad, a doctor, to help her with a complicated experiment on identifying blood types. She and her dad used equipment at the hospital where her dad works, and he ended up doing most of the experiment.

Eleven-year-old Mark and his family just moved into a new house, and he is trying to make friends around the neighborhood. Paul, the neighborhood bully, hassles Mark, teasing him about his thick glasses and calling him a "geek" or "dork" in front of the other kids. Most of the kids seem to like Mark, but when Paul is around, they laugh at Paul's remarks and join in the teasing.

One day after school, Mark went over to Paul's house and asked him to stop making fun of him. At first, Paul laughed at Mark and told

21

him to "get lost." Mark was nervous and intim-
idated, but he calmly told Paul that if the teas-
ing didn't stop right away he would talk to
their parents.

Assertiveness is defined as standing up for yourself or others in honest and appropriate ways that
don't violate another person's rights.[1] What sets
assertiveness apart from the negative aggression we
have been describing is respect for the needs and
rights of others, as well as one's own needs and
rights. In other words, assertiveness is not simply a
way to get something you want; it is a two-way street
where the needs and rights of everyone involved
must be considered before a person acts.

In the examples with Marcia and Mark, it is easy
to tell which young person is using aggression and
which one is being assertive. Marcia lied, cheated,
and used her dad; these are forms of inappropriate
aggression. Her goal was to win first place and beat
her classmate. She might get what she wants, but in
a dishonest way that violates or shows disrespect for
the rights of her classmates, the judges, and her dad.

Mark used assertive behavior in resolving his
issues with Paul, the neighborhood bully. He stood
up for his rights in a direct and honest way while also
respecting Paul's rights. How? Instead of embarrass-
ing Paul in front of the other kids, Mark went to

Paul's house and asked him to stop the teasing. Mark also gave Paul an opportunity to change his behavior before Mark talked to their parents. Mark can get what he wants by doing the right thing.

Many times, a youngster's behavior may appear to be assertive when it actually is inappropriate. Again, the key question in determining whether a youth's behavior is assertive involves appropriate behavior and respecting rights: Is the youngster standing up for his or her rights and needs in honest and appropriate ways that also respect the rights of others? If the answer is "Yes," then the child is being assertive. If the answer is "No," then the child needs to learn more responsible and acceptable ways of getting his or her needs met.

Is Aggression Ever Justified?

So far, we have defined aggression in strictly negative terms. Aggression in children and adolescents is a behavior that parents want to either prevent or reduce as they teach their kids prosocial and positive ways to solve problems or get what they want. There are times, however, when aggressive behavior is both appropriate and necessary. This "justified aggression" can include the use of verbal or physical force, and people most often resort to it in extreme situations where they must act to protect or defend themselves or others.

23

Consider this example: A young girl is walking home from school when a stranger (a man) in a car pulls up to the curb and asks her for directions. When the girl approaches the car, the man suddenly grabs her arm. She reacts by screaming, scratching his face, and eventually biting his hand. The stranger lets go and drives off as the girl runs to the safety of a nearby house.

In this example, the girl was probably thinking that the man was going to kidnap and possibly kill her. This thinking led to feelings of fear, which resulted in the aggressive behaviors of screaming, scratching, and biting. But because she was acting out of self-preservation and self-defense, her actions were justified and appropriate.

Would these same behaviors be justified if the girl attacked her mother because she wouldn't let the girl go to a movie with friends? Absolutely not. In this situation, the girl's thinking might be that her mom is always mean and never fair. This could lead to feelings of anger and frustration, which result in the aggressive behaviors of screaming, scratching, and biting. In this case, the girl's thoughts, feelings, and behaviors would not be justified, and she would likely earn severe negative consequences.

As we said earlier, justified aggression also can be used to protect others. For example, an intruder breaks into a house while a family is sleeping. The father wakes up, grabs a baseball bat, and hits the intruder with it. The father thought the intruder was going to hurt his family, he felt fear and concern for his family's safety, and he responded with aggression. Obviously, the father's thoughts, feelings, and aggressive action were justified and appropriate here because he was protecting himself and his family from harm.

While it is important to point out to parents that children should be taught that they have the right to protect themselves or others by any means possible, we do want to stress that most aggression is undesirable and harmful. Obviously, children can choose to misuse this right, saying that they slugged a classmate on the playground because they felt threatened or in danger. In these situations, parents have to make a judgment call about whether their child's behavior is justified or not, and respond accordingly.

A Serious Problem

As a loving parent, you are concerned about how your children grow up. Besides ensuring their safety, your most important responsibility is to provide the love, discipline, and direction they need in order to become good people. For the most part, you deal only with the behaviors you see your children use. If those behaviors are aggressive in nature, they have an immediate effect that you can see and respond to. In other words, the aggression you are most concerned about is right there at home, and its greatest impact is how it affects you, your child, and the rest of the family.

But aggression in children as a whole affects our entire society. That fact is clear every time you pick up a newspaper or watch television and see stories about young people who decided to solve their problems through violence. For some insight into how serious the problem of youth aggression is, consider these statistics:

- The U.S. Justice Department reported that in 1994 and 1995, a greater proportion of violent crimes was attributed to juveniles than in any of the previous 20 years.

- The Federal Bureau of Investigation (FBI) reported that between 1986 and 1995, there was a 67 percent increase in arrests of juveniles for the crimes of murder and non-negligent manslaughter, forcible rape, robbery, and aggravated assault.

- Research on youth aggression and violence indicates that delinquency rates for youth between 13 and 17 increased 30 percent between 1985 and 1994, and violent crime arrest rates increased 70 percent for persons between the ages of 15 and 18.

The bottom line is that today's youngsters not only are more likely to be involved in acts of delinquency that include aggressive and violent behavior, but also are beginning to commit these acts at younger ages. These acts are increasing across all age groups.

Turning to anger, aggression, and violence as a way of coping with life's challenges can deal a devastating blow to a child's efforts to become a productive and valued member of society. Children who learn and adopt these behaviors have trouble making and keeping friends, and their relationships with parents and siblings can be damaged or destroyed. Adults label them as "troublemakers" or "dangerous" or "delinquents," and eventually, well-intentioned people (teachers, coaches, counselors, youth group leaders, etc.) who want to help, stop trying out of frustration or despair. Instead, they turn their attention to the kids who want to learn and grow. Ultimately, children who choose aggression and violence fail in school, on the playground, in the neighborhood, and at home.

Left unchecked, these harmful behaviors can carry over into adulthood where they can result in spousal and/or child abuse, drug and alcohol abuse, robbery, assault, and other serious criminal activity. These behaviors usually doom the prospects of having a good job, a happy marriage, a loving family, and all of the other things parents want for their children.

The fact that you are reading this book shows that you love your children and are concerned about their prospects for success, now and in the future. You are the most important and influential person in your child's life right now; what you teach about how to get along with people and solve problems becomes his or her road map for life.

When parents know what aggression is and how to deal with it, they can better prepare their children for the journey.

---

[1] Lange, A.J., & Jakubowski, P. (1976). **Responsible assertive behavior: Cognitive/behavioral procedures for trainers.** Champaign, IL: Research Press.

CHAPTER 3

Why Are Kids Aggressive?

Marcus loves candy bars. Whenever he goes to the grocery store with his mom, the 9-year-old can't wait to get to the candy display at the checkout counter. The problem starts when Marcus's mom tells him he can't have a candy bar. First, he begs. Then he gets angry, drops to the floor, and starts screaming. When his mom tries to pull him up, he screams louder and kicks her in the leg. Sometimes, Mom grabs a candy bar from the display counter and shoves it at Marcus just to stop the tantrum. Usually, she ends up trying to push her cart full of groceries out of the store with one hand while dragging Marcus behind her with the other.

Marcus is a child who reacts to situations he doesn't like by getting angry and using aggressive behaviors.

Joyce loves to get her younger brother in trouble. She knows that if she can get him angry over any little thing, her parents will punish him. So she'll stick out her foot to trip him as he walks by her chair or blame him when all the chores don't get done. Sometimes, she'll hide his shoes or clothes just to drive him crazy. And when she really wants something she doesn't want her brother to have (the last cookie or the privilege of riding in the front seat of the car), she threatens to beat him up. Joyce always is careful not to use these behaviors in front of her parents. Joyce is 13, and her brother is 9.

Joyce is a child who thinks about and uses aggressive behaviors to achieve a goal – getting her brother in trouble.

As you can see from these examples, there are two distinct kinds of aggression. One usually involves an angry response and a loss of self-control. When Marcus doesn't get a candy bar, he flips out in front of Mom and the other store customers until he gets what he wants or until Mom drags him out. The other kind of aggression occurs when a child uses negative behaviors to achieve a goal. The child doesn't have to be angry, and the behaviors that are displayed often are planned or thought out ahead of time. Joyce thinks about what she can do to get her brother into trouble. She knows what works and is skillful enough to make him angry without getting in trouble herself.

As we said earlier, the more parents know about aggression, the better equipped they are to help their children reduce or stop using aggressive behaviors. Here, we'll add to your knowledge by presenting a brief look at reactive aggression and planned aggression. There also is a short section on bullying, which is a common form of planned aggression.

Reactive Aggression

Kids who use *reactive aggression* usually *respond* or react to situations they don't like with a lot of emotion. Like Marcus, they are unable to control their temper and can quickly go from being calm to being very angry over minor issues like being told "No" or getting a consequence for misbehaving.

Think about how a 2-year-old might act if he doesn't get his way. There's crying, screaming, and maybe even hitting. It's how kids who haven't learned how to appropriately express their feelings behave in situations where they become angry, frustrated, or fearful. That kind of behavior may be normal for most 2-year-olds, but it's socially unacceptable and inappropriate for an older child or adolescent.

Kids who react with aggression usually don't start with subtle behaviors, but jump directly to more severe types of behavior like yelling, cursing, making verbal threats, punching, or fighting. Generally speaking, these youngsters are not liked by their peers and classmates, and they can be a tremendous source of frustration for parents because no one knows when they might erupt. These kids can be outgoing and gregarious or quiet and passive, but their aggressive response to feelings of anger, frustration, or fear is the same: It's unpredictable and full of emotion.

Planned Aggression

Kids who use *planned aggression* tend to *initiate* aggressive acts. As we said before, these youngsters use aggressive behaviors to achieve a goal, and they often are labeled as "manipulators" or "bullies." (More on bullies later.)

Over time, these youth have learned how to get what they want by using aggressive behaviors. In fact, because their aggressive behavior is planned, they don't necessarily have to be angry or upset. Children who use planned aggression tend to start with lower-level aggressive behaviors and then turn up the heat with more serious behaviors if the minor and subtle ones don't work. For example, if a youngster finds that whining or complaining isn't enough to get her out of doing chores at home, she will resort to more severe behaviors like yelling and cursing. If parents don't recognize this problem and do something to stop it, these kids can jump to the highest levels of aggression, like physically harming others or themselves (Level 4) or using violence (Level 5).

When kids who use planned aggressive behaviors are younger, their peers and classmates do not necessarily dislike them. However, as they get older, other children begin to see them in a more negative light. Like kids who react with aggression, the personalities of youth who use planned aggressive behavior can range from outgoing and sociable to quiet and passive.

Despite these similarities, the key point in determining whether aggression is reactive or planned involves intent. If a child simply reacts, without thinking, to adverse or negative situations by becoming angry and aggressive, it's reactive aggression. If a child intentionally uses aggressive behaviors to achieve a goal, it's planned aggression.

In extreme cases, it is much easier for parents to distinguish between the two types of aggression by looking at whether or not a child is angry and by determining the reason for the aggressive behavior. The task is more difficult with kids who are on the fringes. In either situation, it is important for parents to accurately identify which type of aggression pattern might be developing so they can figure out the best way to reduce or stop it.

Bullying

Everyone has known a bully. He was the kid everyone in the neighborhood feared because he didn't play by any rules. (Girls can be bullies too, but to make this section easier to read, we'll use the pronoun "he.") If the bully wanted something, he took it. If the bully didn't like you, he beat you up or threatened to beat you up. The worst place you could find yourself is alone with the bully and his buddies. (Bullies seem to be meaner and more rotten when they get someone alone, especially when their buddies are around.) The bully usually was bigger than everyone else, and it was a rare occasion when someone stood up to him.

Most of us can look back on our experiences with bullies and remember how afraid we were for ourselves or our friends when the bully was around. If the bully picked on you personally, those times were even more frightening. The good news is that most of us don't have to worry about that experience anymore; the bad news is that bullies are still out there and one of them could live in your home.

Sometimes it's hard to know whether a child is a bully. A kid may be a bully at school, out on the playground, or at the swimming pool, but he rarely uses the aggressive behaviors that keep other kids under his control in front of adults. Again, this is where parents have to be good at identifying and recognizing behaviors that signal that a child is using aggression to get his or her needs met.

Here is a good description of a bully and how he operates. As you read it, think about how his aggressive behaviors are planned and purposeful.

Aaron, a sophomore, is feared by most of the students in his high school – and he likes it that way. Being taller and stronger than most of the other kids, Aaron was the only underclassman to make the cut on the varsity football team, and will likely be a starting player. The coaches praise Aaron, a linebacker on defense, for his ferocious play and brutal hits on opposing players.

Unfortunately, Aaron doesn't leave this "football" behavior on the playing field. In school and in his neighborhood, he uses his size and reputation as a "mean dude" to scare other kids and get them to do what he wants. He thoroughly enjoys badgering and "shaking down" smaller kids for money or other possessions he needs or wants. Recently, Aaron threatened to "kick the crap out" of a younger boy in his neighborhood if the boy didn't give his portable CD player to Aaron. The boy handed it over because he knew from past experience that Aaron wouldn't hesitate to follow through with his threat. The boy was terrified and didn't tell an adult what happened because Aaron threatened to hurt him if he told anyone.

Aaron likes attention. For fun, he often intimidates or forces other kids into doing things that are degrading and humiliating, much to the amusement of the few buddies that hang around with him. For example, during lunch period one day he tried to force another male student to drink a mixture of milk and urine. When the boy refused, Aaron grabbed the boy's hair, held his head up, and poured the concoction into the boy's mouth. Aaron just smiled as his buddies giggled at the "prank." No one – including the victim – reported this incident to a teacher because they were afraid Aaron would get them for "squealing."

Aaron's parents are proud of their son's aggressiveness on the football field. They've always taught him that only people who are strong and tough get what they want, and everyone else is a "wimp." On the rare occasions when other parents have called them to complain about how Aaron has treated their chil-

dren, Aaron's parents have gotten angry, told the other parents to "get a life," and hung up.

How can parents and caregivers determine if a child is a bully? What are some of the characteristics of bullying that parents and caregivers should be aware of that would help them identify a problem? Let's try to answer these questions by first defining what bullying is.

Researchers say bullying is "aggressive behavior or intentional 'harmdoing,' which is carried out repeatedly and over time in an interpersonal relationship characterized by an imbalance of power." Bullying "...often occurs without apparent provocation" and includes negative actions that "...can be carried out by physical contact, by words, or in other ways, such as making faces or mean gestures, and intentional exclusion from a group."[1] Additionally, one of the purposes of bullying is acquiring possessions – money, cigarettes, alcohol, and other things a bully values. In sum, a bully deliberately and repeatedly uses aggression to get what he or she wants from other youngsters who have difficulty defending themselves – physically or emotionally – from the harassment. Bullying, therefore, is considered a form of thought-out aggression.

Studies show that bullies tend to pick on younger and weaker youth, and that the bully/victim relationship can last a long time unless there is some sort of intervention from parents or other adults. Bullies and victims are usually boys, but there is a good deal of bullying that goes on among girls. Whereas boys typically bully kids in physical ways (e.g., pushing, kicking or tripping, punching, etc.), girls tend to use more subtle forms of harassment like keeping someone out of a group, telling lies, trying to turn friends against each other, or trying to stir up trouble between individuals or groups. Parents and other adults often have a difficult time catching on to these behaviors.

Here are some useful facts about bullies:

- Bullies have a positive attitude toward aggression and violence. They enjoy inflicting physical and emotional pain on others and won't hesitate to intimidate and harass others to get what they want.

- Controlling and dominating others – kids and adults – is a strong need that drives a bully's behavior. Bullies like the feelings of power and internal joy they get from controlling others, and they continue to use force and intimidation in order to maintain those feelings.

- Bullies are selfish; everything they do is for their own benefit. The reasons for their behavior are self-centered.

- Bullies are impulsive. If they see something they want, they go after it without thinking about how their aggressive actions affect others or even the consequences to themselves.

- A bully has little, if any, feelings for his or her victims. Bullies simply don't care about the devastating impact their behavior can have on other people's lives.

- Contrary to popular belief, bullies do not suffer from low self-esteem. Surprisingly, the opposite is true: Bullies have little anxiety and are very secure in their identity.

- There is an imbalance of power between a bully and his victim. A typical victim is unable to defend himself or herself – physically or emotionally – from a bully's harassment.

- For bullies who engage in extremely violent acts (e.g., assault, rape, murder, etc.), there is easy access to a deadly weapon, like a knife or a gun.

Whatever form bullying takes – from simple verbal harassment to physical violence – it creates a harmful situation for both the bully and the victim. Children and adolescents who learn to rely on the use of force to get what they want will fail in a society where positive, appropriate social interaction between people is a key to success. In extreme cases, this failure can include alienation, criminal activity and incarceration, and an absence of meaningful relationships. For the victim, there is the immediate fear, humiliation, and pain of being singled out for abuse, as well as possible long-lasting effects like loss of self-confidence or a feeling of inferiority. Some victims of bullies also tend to become or remain victims in other areas of their lives as they mature.

Believe it or not, some adults might not see anything seriously wrong with the behavior of bullies. They might take a "boys will be boys" attitude, arguing that it's normal for bigger and stronger kids to control the smaller, weaker kids. Some people might even blame the victims for being too weak or timid to stand up for themselves. What these folks fail to see is that being bigger and stronger and meaner doesn't entitle anyone to demean, belittle, embarrass, harass, or hurt other people. Bullying is wrong, plain and simple, and adults should intervene to stop such behavior when they become aware of it.

Parents also must teach their children not to tolerate bullies. In situations where a bully poses a problem, there are three groups of youth: the bullies, the victims, and the bystanders. Bystanders are the kids whom the bully doesn't bother. When victims can't protect or stand up for themselves, it is sometimes up to the bystanders to step in and do something. That might involve telling an adult – a parent, a teacher, a counselor, a coach – about what's going on. It also might require the bystanders to put some pressure on the bully to leave the victims alone. This takes a certain amount of courage and assertiveness, and parents should talk to their children about the importance of helping other people who are being harassed or harmed. We are not advocating that parents tell their children to fight a bully or put themselves in a dangerous situation. But group pressure can be very powerful, and kids should know that protecting themselves and their friends is the right thing to do.

In the first three chapters of this book we have talked about the importance of being able to recognize aggression in children and the many types of behaviors that can tip off parents to a problem. In the next few chapters, we'll discuss what you can do as a parent to prevent or deal with aggressive behavior, including how to create a safe, healthy home and how to teach your child positive ways to get along with others and solve problems.

---

[1] Olweus, D. (1996) Bullying at school: Knowledge base and an effective intervention program. In T. Grisso & C.F. Fernis (Eds.), **Understanding aggressive behavior in children** (pp. 265-276). New York: The New York Academy of Sciences.

What Parents
Can Do

CHAPTER 4

Set a
Good Example

Being a parent is tough. Taking on the responsibility of caring for, worrying about, teaching, and unconditionally loving a human being whose present and future life depend on your love, skill, and knowledge is an awesome chore. To make the job even more difficult, parents must combat a multitude of outside forces that seem bent on undoing or ruining everything good they try to do for their children.

As we said earlier, aggression most often is a learned trait. Most children and adolescents who display aggressive or violent behaviors have seen these behaviors somewhere and made them their own. These kids either have not been taught that such behavior is wrong and that there are positive ways to behave instead, or they've failed to learn that lesson.

Do parents intentionally teach their children to use force and intimidation to settle differences and obtain possessions? In most families, the answer is "No." Do parents sometimes permit their children to be exposed to influences that can allow or even promote the development of aggressive behavior? In many families, the answer to this question might be "Yes." Parents either are using the very behaviors they want their kids to avoid, or don't know what their children are learning or who they are learning it from. Whatever the situation, children who grow up surrounded by aggression and violence are likely to become aggressive and violent themselves.

It is painfully obvious that our society has become more violent and more dangerous. How far off track have we gotten? A simple disagreement can lead to a fistfight. If someone cuts you off in traffic, you don't dare look at the other driver for fear that he or she may have a gun. And think about what we see every day in the media. Stories about murder and mayhem dominate the newspaper headlines. Many television newsrooms live by the motto, "If it bleeds, it leads." Guests on talk shows "discuss" their problems by throwing punches and chairs. Movies are two-hour collections of bloody gunfights and thundering explosions, and sporting events are marred by brawls, disrespect or disdain for the rules and officials, and vulgar language. Should we be surprised that more young people are turning to aggression and violence to get what they want and settle disputes when kids see that very kind of behavior every day?

Parents must combat the many negative influences children face, both inside and outside the home. To do this, parents must create for kids a healthy environment that promotes positive values and behaviors. Boys Town believes there are two parts to accomplishing this goal. The first part focuses on common-sense ways to shape positive behavior in children. Shaping behavior involves gradually introducing new behaviors and practicing them, and eliminating negative influences that foster negative behavior. Making those kinds of changes is what the next several chapters are about; they offer some effective strategies for creating a home environment that emphasizes positive behavior. The second part involves different kinds of teaching that parents can use to help their children make healthy choices when it comes to getting along with others or getting something they want. Chapters 11 through 14 will discuss those teaching methods in detail.

As you read the rest of this book, keep in mind that prevention and early intervention are the keys to reducing or stopping aggressive behaviors. Ignoring the problem or hoping it will go away doesn't work and can set the stage for worse behaviors. Remember that it is easier to catch and fix negative behaviors before they become serious. Working together with your child can build or repair relationships and strengthen the bond that must exist in a loving parent-child relationship.

The next section and the following chapters describe ways parents can bring about change in their homes and families. You may already be using some of them. If so, keep up the good work. If you realize there is more you can do to protect your children, start making some changes today. As a parent, you know there are no guarantees when it comes to rearing children. But when young people have positive experiences and images to draw from, they're more likely to make better decisions about their behavior.

When Seth came up to bat in the bottom of the last inning, there were two outs and his Little League team was behind 5-4. Seth was nervous. His teammate, Brian, was on third base, and Seth knew he had to get a hit to tie the score.

Seth's dad also was nervous. This was the biggest game of the year, and as the coach of Seth's team, he was proud of how his boys had played. Now his son had a chance to be a hero.

The pitcher wound up and fired a fast ball down the middle. Seth swung and hit a hard grounder to the right side of the infield. The second baseman bobbled the ball, then threw to first base. The ball smacked into the first baseman's glove a half second before Seth's foot hit the base.

"You're out!" bellowed the umpire. Game over.

Seth's dad charged out of the dugout, heading toward first base. The umpire stiffened, expecting the coach to argue the call. But the coach rushed past the umpire to Seth, put his arm around his son, and said, "That was a good hard hit and good hustle. You did your best and that's all you can do. We'll get them next time." Then he lined up his players to shake hands with the other team.

Out in the parking lot, Seth and his dad saw the umpire getting into his car. Seth's dad walked over, shook hands with the umpire, and told him he had called a good game. On the way home, Seth asked his dad if he was mad because the umpire called Seth out.

"No, because it was a good call," Dad replied. "Besides, the umpire was doing the best he could, just like you."

Modeling simply means consistently using positive behaviors in front of your children. Whether you realize it or not, your kids are always watching and listening to you. Setting a good example is one of the single most important ways parents can teach their children positive behaviors.

In the story about Seth, Seth's dad could have used all kinds of aggressive behaviors. He could have gotten mad because his son was called out and his team lost. He could have argued with the umpire over the call at first base or even attacked the umpire. (This happens more often than most parents would want to admit.) Seth's dad also could have stalked off the field without shaking hands with the other team. But he didn't do any of those things. Even though he was disappointed, Seth's dad accepted what happened and praised the way his son and his team played. And in a wonderful act of sportsmanship, he shook hands with the umpire afterwards in the parking lot.

Seth saw all this. And he'd probably seen his dad act the same way throughout the season. What lessons do you think Seth learned about sportsmanship and getting along with others from watching his dad?

If your child is using aggressive behaviors, look at your own behaviors. Are you sending the right message to your kids by how you express anger or deal with someone who does something you don't like? Are you setting a good example? Remember that your kids look up to you and try to be like you. If they see that you can stay calm when you are angry and can resolve disagreements or get what you want in positive ways, they are more likely to try to do the same.

If you are modeling good behaviors and your child still uses aggressive or other negative behaviors, outside forces could be disrupting your efforts. For instance, instead of following your example, your kids might be imitating friends or peers, or people or characters they've seen on TV or in movies, who model bad behavior. Check who your kids are hanging out with and what kinds of TV shows and movies they're watching, and make whatever changes are necessary. That might mean helping your child find new friends or putting some restrictions on what programs he or she watches. When people outside your family are having a bigger impact on your child's behavior then you are, that's a major problem. It's time to sit down with your child and specifically review and explain your expectations and rules for appropriate behavior. Consistently modeling good behavior works only if the example you set is the one your kids choose to follow.

CHAPTER 5

Watch What Your Kids Watch

Miranda watches television for hours at a time. Her favorite programs are talk shows where guests talk about their problems, get into arguments, and end up punching and kicking each other. When her TV programs aren't on, she pops in a movie from her large collection of "teen slasher" films. Although Miranda and most of her friends are only 14, they regularly attend R-rated movies that are heavy on violence, foul language, and sex. In her room, Miranda keeps stacks of violent comic books, and the walls are adorned with posters that have satanic themes.

Miranda's parents think she's just "going through a phase." They see no harm in the movies, TV shows, books, and posters she likes, *and even have bought some of the videotapes as presents. (Mom and Dad have never watched the movies.) Miranda gets good grades in school and seems to get along well with other people. However, her teachers have told Miranda's parents that on one occasion, they overheard Miranda and her friends talking about what it would be like to kill someone. When her parents confronted her about these conversations, Miranda said she and her girlfriends were just joking around.*

Is Miranda at risk to develop aggressive behaviors? Definitely. She seems to be infatuated with "entertainment" that has violent themes, and her parents don't seem to mind. While Miranda might not be displaying serious aggressive behaviors, the fact that she has discussed what it would be like to cause someone's death is a clear sign that she is being dangerously influenced by the messages she's getting from the media.

It is impossible in this technological age for anyone to be completely isolated from the media. Television, radio, movies, books, magazines, music tapes and compact discs, newspapers, artwork, and billboards are almost everywhere, bombarding us with messages that inform, entertain, sell a product, or make a statement. Some of the messages carried by the media are positive and educational; others are negative or downright dangerous.

It is up to parents to decide what is right or wrong for their child to see, hear, or read. They know their children best and know what their child can handle and understand. Parents are the ones who have to set the boundaries for their children's exposure to media messages. When children have no guidance, they can be easily influenced by the harmful messages.

While there are many forms of media, the four we consider to have the most influence on kids today are television, movies, music, and the computer.

Television is a fixture in the lives of most children. It can serve as a baby sitter, a teacher, an entertainer, and a shaper of behavior. Unfortunately, the effects it can have are not always positive. Recent research indicates that kids who watch a lot of television programs with violent material are more likely to use violent behaviors with others than kids who aren't exposed to those kinds of programs. And since research shows that kids watch about 30 hours of TV a week, it's a pretty good bet that they'll see some programs with violent content.

Even worse may be the way kids become desensitized to violence. In other words, children become unable to feel compassion or sympathy for people who are killed or hurt in real life because they have seen so many characters get shot, stabbed, blown up, or "killed" some other way on television. In fact, studies on children's viewing habits have found that the average child will witness more than 8,000 murders on television before age 12.

Violent movies have the same impact. Story lines are built around conflict, and conflict is usually settled with force and graphic violence, the gorier the better. Kids laugh and cheer when the hero blows the villain to pieces with a rocket launcher. They shriek with delight when the killer leaps out of a closet and stabs a screaming teen-age girl. And they rate how "cool" a movie is by its body count and the number of gunshots and explosions. Even movies that are rated PG or PG-13 can contain violent scenes that many parents would find objectionable for younger children.

Music also is very influential, especially among teenagers. Radio stations play songs that are heavy on lyrics about death, suicide, violence (mainly against women), and aggression. Young people can buy tapes and CDs with objectionable material, even though many now carry warning labels. Teens idolize rock stars who promote a lifestyle of violence, drugs, and sex. A number of music videos also have violent themes, and a style of music called "gangsta' rap" relies heavily on profanity to describe, and sometimes glorify, gang violence.

Finally, computers have opened up a whole new world of experiences – good and bad – for young people. The Internet is great for doing research for reports, but kids also can easily access websites that contain violent or pornographic material. And state-of-the-art computer games continually push the envelope in terms of mayhem and gore, especially those in which players participate in bloody virtual shootouts with a variety of "enemies."

What can parents do to protect their children from these negative influences? First, they can filter the images and messages that are available to kids. This means knowing the content of and monitoring what kids watch on television, what movies they go to, what kinds of music they listen to, what kinds of books and magazines they read, and what they pull up on the Internet or play on the computer.

So check out the television programs your kids watch and the movies they want to see. Monitoring the television is easiest; it's in your home so you can usually see what your kids are watching, and you can check out the maturity rating for programs ahead of time. Set limits for how much TV your kids can watch. As we mentioned earlier, the average child watches about 30 hours of television a week; that's more than double the maximum of 14 hours a week experts recommend. For movies, read reviews in the newspaper or magazines, or pull up information about films on the Internet. This can give you a good idea of what the movie is about and whether there is graphic violence or sex or inappropriate language. If possible, view a movie before letting your child see it. Then you can make an informed decision about whether you want your child to see it.

Listen to some of the music your child likes. Find out something about the artists or groups, especially if you suspect that the lyrics are not appropriate for children and teens. Also, check out song lyrics and find out why certain CDs and tapes carry warning labels. (Lyrics often are printed on inserts that come with a CD or tape.) The more information you have, the better decisions you and your child can make about what kind of music you want in your home.

If you have a computer in your home and are connected to the Internet, find out what websites your kids are visiting. Also check out the computer games your child might be playing. (Play them yourself.) Monitor what your child is doing on the computer, even if it's in his or her room. Awareness is the key here; if you don't know your child is doing something that is potentially harmful, you can't take steps to stop it.

Second, parents can talk to their kids about what they see or hear. For example, if you're watching a TV show together and there's a shooting, ask questions like, "How do think it would feel if a person really got shot?" or "What would really happen if someone shot someone?" or "Is that the way people should treat each other?" This helps kids understand that TV shows and movies are play-acting, and that people actually get hurt or die as a result of real-life violence.

This also is a great opportunity to talk about how people who use violence and aggression in real life face serious consequences, like being arrested and going to jail. For example, children see many television programs and movies where the "hero" seeks revenge. Usually, the plot involves a bad guy who hurts or kills someone who is the good guy's friend, wife, husband, brother, etc. Then the good guy sets out on a mission to even the score. No matter how the good guy gets back at the bad guy, it is portrayed as being justified and right, and the "hero" rarely faces any negative consequences for his actions. (A study found that the "good guys" initiate about 40 percent of the violent acts seen on television, and that the consequences of violent behavior are shown only 15 percent of the time.) Children, especially young kids, must understand that using violence to get back at someone who has "dissed" or hurt them or someone they like rarely is the right thing to do, and that such behavior can carry a heavy punishment.

Third, do a lot of teaching so your children know what you consider to be appropriate and inappropriate material. As a parent, you can help shape your child's view of the world; if you consistently reinforce the idea that using violence and aggression is not the way to solve problems, he or she will be more likely to buy into that idea and make it part of his or her own belief system. This makes it easier for a child to understand the difference between fantasy violence and reality violence and make better choices in situations where he or she becomes angry or frustrated.

Finally, remember that you control what comes into your house, whether it's through the airwaves or the Internet, or from the video or music store. You can make certain television shows, movies, music, comic books, computer games, and Internet sites off limits because they are inappropriate for children. Discuss your decisions with your kids so they understand your point of view. If your kids are home alone a lot, you can make rules for using the computer, and set limits on how much television and the types of programs they can watch when you're gone. You also can look into blocking objectionable TV programs and Internet sites so that your kids don't have access to them.

If your kids have a lot of free time, have them do chores, read, write letters to grandma or grandpa, or have friends over to play. Many kids think that watching television and enjoying other forms of entertainment is a God-given right. It's not. For example, there's nothing wrong with having your kids earn their TV time; then the television becomes a privilege rather than an electronic baby-sitter that's always blaring in the background.

CHAPTER 6

Teach Problem-Solving

When children have a positive way to solve their problems or figure out how to get what they want, they are less likely to turn to aggression. Boys Town has developed a problem-solving method that is easy for parents to teach and easy for kids to learn.

This method is called **SODAS**. The letters stand for **Situation, Options, Disadvantages, Advantages,** and **Solution.** SODAS is a good method because it helps accomplish two goals:

- It gives parents and children a process for solving problems and making decisions together.

- It helps parents teach children how to solve problems and make decisions on their own.

Here is how SODAS works:

Situation – Before you can solve a problem, you must know what the problem is. Ask your child to describe the situation. This step usually takes the longest because kids often use vague or emotional descriptions. You can help by asking open-ended questions like, "What did you do then?" or "What happened next?" Avoid questions that kids can answer with a "Yes" or a "No," or a word that really doesn't mean much like "Fine." The goal here is to define the situation as clearly as possible so the child can come up with the best solution.

It's also a good idea to summarize the information your child provides. Children sometimes become so emotional when talking about a problem that they lose sight of what the actual problem is. Once you've stated the problem in its simplest form, ask the child if your summary is correct.

Options – Oftentimes, kids see a solution as an "all-or-nothing" deal. For example, a child who isn't getting along with a neighbor boy might think that moving out of the neighborhood is the only solution. But every problem usually has several options for solutions. So have your child write down three to four options. Don't make any comments on whether they are good or bad, or whether they will work or not; the purpose here is to get the child to think of ways to make his or her own decision. If your child has trouble coming up with options, make some suggestions to get him or her started.

Disadvantages/Advantages – In this step, you help your child look at the pros and cons of each option. This helps the child see the connection between each option and what could happen if that option is chosen.

First, ask your child for his or her thoughts about each option. (What's good about the option? What's bad? Why would the option work? Why won't the option work?) Then help him or her come up with a list of disadvantages and advantages for each one. Write these down so you both can remember them.

Solution – Now it's time for your child to pick an option to try. Quickly summarize the advantages and disadvantages for each option, and have your child choose the one that he or she thinks will work best. Make sure your child knows the options and the possible outcomes of each one. If a decision doesn't have to be made right away, let your child take some time to think about his or her choice. Once the choice is made, you can help him or her practice using the solution. If the solution involves having your child talk to someone, you can play the part of the other person and respond to what your child says in ways the other person might. This prepares the child for a variety of responses.

After your child tries the solution he or she picked, check later to see if it worked. This is an excellent time to praise your child for making a decision and following through with it.

A few words of caution: Children sometimes may come up with or want to try options that you don't agree with. In those situations, the general rule is that if the option won't hurt anyone and isn't illegal or contrary to your moral or religious beliefs, then let the child make the choice and learn from his or her decision.

If this process is new to you, begin with a small problem. This gives your child time to feel comfortable with using it. Many kids don't have the patience to think things out. They get frustrated and just want to get it over with. But don't let your kids make quick choices; teach them that it's worth taking some extra time to come up with a solution that works and doesn't involve aggressive behaviors.

While you will want to encourage your kids to make decisions and solve problems on their own, you need to let them know that you will always be there to help and support them. If a solution does not work out as planned, go back to the SODAS method and find another solution to the problem.

CHAPTER 7

Know Where Your Kids Are

We've already discussed the importance of monitoring the TV programs and movies your kids see, the music they listen to, the books they read, and the Internet sites they visit. Now let's talk about a different kind of monitoring, one that involves keeping track of your kids' behaviors, who they hang around with, what's happening at school, what they do with their free time, and how they see the world around them.

Whether your kids are younger or older, monitoring their activities lets them know that you care about them and their safety. In fact, it's a good idea to remind your children from time to time that you want to know what they're involved in because you love them. If kids don't understand your reasons, they might think that all you're doing is spying on them, a situation that can cause mistrust and bad feelings.

As we said earlier, you are the biggest influence in your child's life. If you don't know what your kids are doing and aren't involved in their lives (aside from making sure they have a roof over their heads and food on the table), someone else may take over that role. When that someone is another youth (or a group of youths) who are up to no good, trouble could be just around the corner.

Checking on your kids is a great way to help them avoid negative peer pressure. When you know what's going on, you can help your children head off problems before they occur by teaching them how to make good decisions when someone tries to talk them into doing something harmful or destructive. Kids can become very confused when they're being pulled in different directions by parents and teachers on one side and their friends and peers on the other. They often will need to sort through a mess of thoughts and feelings, and informed parents are better able to help their kids make good decisions.

Monitoring also provides you with more opportunities to catch your kids being good and to reward them for good behavior. This reinforces positive behaviors and makes it more likely that your kids will use them in the future. (See Chapter 14.)

Obviously, talking with your kids at meals, bedtime, or when you're just sitting around is the best way to keep up with what's going on in their lives. But you can't be with your kids every minute, especially when they go out. You need to know what they're doing outside the home. So get to know your child's friends, and set and enforce rules and curfews for going out. One parent who had four teenagers came up with a great way to take care of these situations. She posted a note on the refrigerator (a spot she knew the kids would visit often). The note read: "Before you ask me to go anywhere, be prepared to tell me where you are going, how you'll get there and back, when you'll be home, what you'll be doing, and who you'll be with." This parent had a pretty good idea of what her kids were doing when they weren't at home. Parents also can make a point of talking with their kids when they get home about what happened while they were gone. This should be a conversation, not a confrontation or an interrogation. Kids have to know that you trust them, and even when they make mistakes (and they will), they have to know that you love them.

CHAPTER 8

Teach Ahead
of Time

D ante and Tony are friends, but they don't
always get along. In the past, the two 10-
year-olds have had some pretty good fights over
who gets to play on the swing first or who was
ahead in one of their driveway basketball games.
Recently, Dante's dad and Tony's dad decided to
try something new: Before their sons get together to play, each dad sits down with his son and
talks about how the boys are expected to behave.
Specifically, the dads teach their sons how to act
if the boys have a disagreement. Both dads tell
their sons how they can settle their differences
calmly, without fighting. They also tell the boys
that if they can't do that, they are to come home.
When the boys play without fighting, they both
get to do something fun with their dads. If the

boys fight, they have to help clean the house. In the two weeks since the teaching started, the boys have had only one fight.

The dads in the example are using a method that Boys Town calls **Proactive Teaching**. It's very simple, and it works. In fact, you've probably already used a form of it with your own child. Think about the times you told your child how to safely cross the street, how to call 911, and how to be careful near a hot stove. You were trying to prevent problems by telling your child what to do before your child encountered a specific situation. That's Proactive Teaching.

Proactive Teaching is defined as describing to a child what he or she should do in a future situation and practicing it in advance. It is most effective when your child is learning something new or when he or she has had difficulty in a past situation. Though it can be used in many areas, it is an especially good tool for helping kids learn positive ways (learning something new) to respond in situations where they have resorted to aggressive behaviors in the past.

Proactive Teaching combines clear messages about what behavior is expected, kid-related reasons for using the behavior, and practice. Teaching should occur before a child faces a new situation or a situation where he or she has had difficulty. It's best to use

Proactive Teaching when your child is calm and attentive, not after a misbehavior or when he or she is upset.

Here are the three steps to Proactive Teaching. Each step is followed by an example of what it would sound like if Dante's dad (in the earlier example) was using it with Dante.

Step 1. Describe the behavior you would like to see.

"Dante, can I talk with you for a minute? I know you're going over to Tony's house to play. If you and Tony start to argue, stay calm and try to work out the problem without fighting. Okay? If you feel like you can't stay calm, come home right away."

Step 2. Give a reason.

"If you can work things out without fighting, you'll have more time to play. And you won't have to come home sooner than you want."

Step 3. Practice.

"Okay, before you go, let's practice. Pretend I'm Tony and I just told you that I want the ball first when we play basketball. Tell me what could you say?" (Dante says it's okay if Tony takes the ball first.) "Great! That's the way to prevent an argument. And

you can take the ball first for the next game. Now go have fun."

Children won't always have the right answer or know what they should do. In this example, Dante might not know what he should say when he and Tony argue over the basketball. In this situation, Dante's dad could handle the practice step this way:

"Okay, before you go, let's practice. Pretend I'm Tony and I just told you that I want the ball first when we play basketball. Tell me what could you say?" (Dante says he doesn't know.) *"That's all right. I'll help you. What about letting Tony have the ball first and then taking turns after that? Would that be better than arguing?"* (Dante nods.) *"Okay. Tell me again what you should say?"* (Dante says he could let Tony have the ball first.) *"There you go! You've got it! And you can take the ball first for the next game. Now go have fun."*

Proactive Teaching only works if you remember to use it. When you do a lot of teaching, you not only frequently remind the child about the expected behavior but also provide more opportunities for him or her to practice it. And don't get discouraged. You may have to practice a dozen times before your child learns what you are trying to teach and begins to use it consistently. Don't expect perfection right away. It took your child some time to learn the negative behaviors you're trying to change, and it will take some time to learn the new ones.

After finishing the practice, praise your child for what he or she did well and encourage your child to improve in areas where he or she can do better. If you are practicing a complex skill or what to do in a difficult situation, never promise that the situation will work out perfectly. Remind your child that he or she is practicing possible ways to handle a situation and that the outcome won't always be the same as the one that's practiced. You cannot ensure your children's success, but you can improve the odds that they will succeed.

CHAPTER 9

Set Boundaries and Rules

Setting boundaries on what behaviors you will allow your children to use accomplishes two goals: It lets your children know exactly what you consider to be acceptable and unacceptable behavior, and it establishes a tolerance level – how far you let your child's inappropriate behaviors go before you step in to stop them.

It is best to set low tolerances, especially when you are trying to prevent or deal with aggression. Low tolerances put limits on what your children can and cannot do. For example, parents with low tolerances would intervene when their kids start arguing instead of waiting until they are on the floor fighting. When children understand that their parents won't tolerate certain behaviors and that stepping over the line will result in negative consequences, they are less likely to use those behaviors.

It is important when setting low tolerances to explain them to your kids. Much of the time, your tolerances are conveyed through how you describe inappropriate behavior or behaviors you would like to see to your child. They also come through in the consequences you give for inappropriate behavior. Be careful here. Constantly reminding, nagging, or badgering your child about his or her problem behaviors can damage a relationship and bring out aggressive behavior. A balanced approach, where you address misbehavior when necessary and maintain a good relationship with your kids, usually works best.

Talking with your children about what behaviors are acceptable, and consistently following through with consequences when unacceptable behaviors occur, also gives kids a clear picture of what you expect from them. So say what you mean, and mean what you say. Be brief and consistent when correcting or disciplining a misbehavior, avoid nagging, and explain your tolerances ahead of time so your kids won't get into the habit of constantly questioning what you do.

Most families have rules that everyone is expected to follow. Rules are important because they set the boundaries for what is acceptable behavior and what is not. This is what keeps a household from falling into chaos. While parents are in charge of enforcing the rules, the entire family can be involved in deciding what they are. Here are our suggested Top Ten rules for helping to prevent or reduce aggression or aggressive behaviors. (You may be able to come up with others to meet your family's needs.)

1. **No hitting or kicking** – No one is allowed to physically strike anyone else.

2. **No swearing** – No one is allowed to use vulgar, profane, or obscene language.

3. **No temper tantrums** – If someone becomes upset, the person is to go to his or her room until he or she is calm.

4. **No threats** – No one is allowed to threaten another person, either verbally or physically.

5. **Do something nice** – Each family member must do something nice for at least one other family member every day. (This may not be possible when a family member is away from home for a few days.)

6. **Don't talk back** – Children must listen without interrupting when a parent or another adult is talking. If a child wants to respond, he or she must ask permission and then talk in an appropriate voice tone (no yelling, whining, etc.).

7. **Cooperate** – Family members should do chores, solve problems, and make decisions together.

(Some decisions should be made only by parents, but many can involve the whole family.)

8. **Show respect** – Everyone in the family should treat each other with respect. This means remembering that mom, dad, sister, brother, and any other family member who lives in the home are the most important people in the world.

9. **Show love** – Everyone should take time each day to tell other family members how much they're loved. Affectionate gestures like hugs, kisses, and pats on the back are always a good idea.

10. **Live the Golden Rule** – The Golden Rule tells us to treat others the way we want to be treated. This is the key to getting along with others.

Simply writing down these rules and posting them where everyone can see them is not enough. First, all family members should be aware of the rules and understand what each one means. Then, parents must take the responsibility of enforcing the rules. The best way to do that is through consequences and praise.

Consequences can be positive or negative. They can be planned out ahead of time so everyone – especially the kids – knows what to expect when they follow a rule or break a rule. The most effective positive consequences are things that people like or want. Negative consequences that work best are things that people don't like or want to avoid. For example, 7-year-old Bob likes to play cards with Mom. So if Bob does something nice for his sister, he knows that he can earn 15 minutes of playing cards with Mom. On the other hand, Bob doesn't like to help do the dishes. So he knows that if he talks back to Dad, he will earn two extra times to help with the dishes.

We'll talk more about consequences in the next few chapters. For now, it's important to remember that consequences can help change behaviors. It's also essential to understand that consequences that involve physical punishment, or words or actions that demean, embarrass, or otherwise tear down a child's self-esteem and confidence are not appropriate and are not effective in the long run. Using consequences should be part of a plan that teaches children new behaviors in a positive manner.

CHAPTER 10

Create a Strong Spiritual Foundation

This chapter is a brief introduction to the central role that religion plays in helping children and families build happy, successful lives together. Most books about parenting either only give lip service to the healing power of religion or make it a total explanation for everything. At Boys Town, we find a middle ground between these two extremes.

As a parent, you have an opportunity and responsibility to help your children learn and understand that their lives will not make sense without a strong religious foundation. This foundation includes living a life of strong personal faith and public worship. This is especially true in situations where aggression needs to be prevented or reduced in the lives of children.

81

Boys Town's founder, Father Edward Flanagan, was fond of saying: "Every boy (or girl) must learn to pray." Today in America this is not considered politically correct. However, basing moral norms on the majority opinion of a society is perilous indeed. It does not fill our children with the private virtue they must have in order to flourish. A boy or girl who fights, lies, cheats, steals, acts out sexually, or hurts others will not be successful. Father Flanagan was right. Every boy and girl must learn to pray.

What can parents do to create an atmosphere that will enable children and families to grow in faith and morality? Here are a few suggestions:

1. Be a role model of faith yourself.

As a parent, you have to be a person of deep faith. And you have to sincerely and constantly model your faith for your children, not just when you want them to see it and imitate it. Your attitude toward life – what you say and what you do – is a sign that your children pick up on. It isn't enough for you to attend church every Sunday as a family. Parents have to live their faith the rest of the week as well.

2. Teach your child to pray regularly.

Prayer should be part of your family's daily routine. Remember that "the family that prays together, stays together."

- Pray before meals.
- Pray in the morning.
- Pray before bedtime.
- Pray for sick relatives and friends.
- Pray prayers of thanksgiving.
- Pray prayers of blessing.

Teach your children how to pray by praying with them. Then help them memorize important prayers. Stress that prayer is important, not because it will get them what they want, but because it is a way of developing their relationship with God.

Consider this simple comparison. If you want to develop a relationship with someone, you engage them in conversation and do things together that are fun, helpful, caring, and sharing. If your child wants to have a relationship with God, he or she must engage Him in conversations of prayer, both in private and in public, and in activities. Teaching your children to read the Bible also is important. And you begin by reading it yourself.

3. Be sure your children attend religious services.

Of course, you need to attend services with your children. If you "send" your children to church and insist that they go, and then don't go yourself, you communicate this message to them: Church is important when you are young; it is not important when you are an adult. That is not the message you want to send.

One of the hardest things for 21st century people to understand is the need for other people. As a society, we have become so concerned about our own needs that we sometimes overlook the nourishing power the community can have on us. Taking part in community events is species specific. Community prayer is important if we are to flourish as human beings. Keeping your children from church increases their sense of loneliness and isolation.

Remember that you should try to avoid extremes in your public worship. Worship is not entertainment, and it is not a chore. Participating in worship and prayer strengthens an individual and a family, helps create a common bond of faith, and gives children the moral and spiritual underpinnings that encourage them to treat others with kindness and respect.

4. Encourage your child to participate in activities that promote spiritual growth.

Here are some good places to start:
- Church youth groups

- Bible study classes
- Sunday school
- Summer church camp

These are all great ways for young people to meet each other and share their faith. These types of experiences strengthen youngsters and help them gain insight into the importance of their spiritual life.

5. Teach your children the Ten Commandments.

There is a way to do this that works well. Let's take the example of stealing, which would pertain to the Eighth Commandment. First, ask your child why God said we should not steal. When kids look inside themselves for the answer, they find that:

- They don't like it when people steal from them.
- Other people don't like it when someone steals from them.
- It is hard to live in a family and a home where people steal from each other.
- It is impossible to care and share when people rip each other off. (That includes shoplifting.)
- It is impossible to have a happy life when people cheat each other.

If children can find reasons inside themselves for why they shouldn't steal, then they can understand why God wrote a rule against stealing that is outside of all of us. God teaches us that stealing is wrong in two ways: by speaking to us from the inside and by making rules on the outside.

This lesson is true for each of the Commandments.

- In our heart of hearts, we don't want to be lied to.

- In our heart of hearts, we want to treat our neighbor as we want to be treated.

6. Do community service or charity work with your child.

This is another way of living your faith. It can be a powerful moment when a child learns the meaning of charity while helping to serve food at a homeless shelter, visiting the sick, or making a cake for someone who has experienced a death in the family.

Doing something for someone out of kindness (and not for some personal reward) can be one of the most fulfilling experiences a child or an adult can have.

7. Teach your child to practice random acts of kindness.

These can be as simple as holding the door open for someone or giving up your seat to an elderly person. It's a random act of kindness for a child to say, "Mom, that was a very good meal tonight. Thank you very much."

If children can learn the skills of caring and sharing (without worrying about rewards), there is a better chance that they will continue to choose positive, helpful behavior over hurtful, violent behavior.

Putting these suggestions to work in your family can help you achieve many spiritual goals with your children. Here are eight important goals:

1. Help each child appreciate and cherish his or her fundamental relationship with God.

2. Help each child become a role model of faith for others.

3. Have each child attend worship services regularly.

4. Help each child learn more about his or her faith.

5. Help each child to become a person who prays regularly and appreciates the religious significance of special events like Christmas, Hanukkah, Passover, Easter, Thanksgiving, birthdays, Baptismal days, and other personal milestones.

6. Help each child develop sound, solid religious habits at home.

7. Help each child develop a positive relationship with clergy.

8. Help each child develop a balanced spiritual life, one that is not overexaggerated or underexaggerated.

Spiritual growth is an essential part of every child's life, as important as physical, emotional, social, and academic growth. Without spiritual growth, none of the other areas will mean much. Parents give their children a great gift when they teach them how to develop as spiritual beings with a sense of God-given purpose. In our society, being strong in faith is not always popular. But it should be. If we are to teach our children – the next generation – how to build good, moral lives in a good, moral society, we must share with them our own faith experiences and practices. Believing in God, and living our lives according to His plan, is at the heart of goodness. It is our call to treat others with love and compassion rather than hatred and anger.

Teach Your Children Well

CHAPTER 11

When Children Misbehave

When it comes right down to it, the biggest part of parenting is teaching. Parents face no greater challenge than instilling in their children the knowledge and skills they will need for life.

Much of the teaching parents do is in response to a child's misbehavior. This is difficult enough, but the task becomes even harder when a parent is trying to prevent or deal with aggressive or violent behaviors. Parents need a proven, effective plan of action.

Boys Town has found that the best plan for teaching has both structure and flexibility. Structure is necessary to ensure that the information you want a child to have is given clearly and effectively. It also ensures that teaching is consistent and that children can become accustomed to and comfortable with it.

Flexibility allows parents to use this structured teaching in many different situations and to modify how they teach so their kids get the most out of it. It also helps parents to teach "naturally." That means teaching is not forced or artificial, but rather is a part of the normal give-and-take that occurs between parents and children every day.

Not all parents know how to respond to their children's misbehaviors with teaching that combines this structure and flexibility. In fact, many parents have told us that when they try to correct their children, they do something different each time or they end up yelling and arguing. This may work to stop the misbehavior temporarily, but it doesn't teach why the behavior is wrong and what the child should do instead. This isn't healthy for the parent or the child because the child does not develop necessary life skills, the parent becomes frustrated, and the relationship between the two suffers. When this situation exists in a family where a child is developing aggressive tendencies, it also can be physically harmful for the child, family members, and people outside the family. Concerned parents want a constructive, effective way to respond when their children misbehave. Boys Town offers a five-step process called **Corrective Teaching**.

Corrective Teaching works best in situations where children are doing something they shouldn't do or are not doing something they should do. A few of those specific situations include:

- Not following instructions.
- Doing something that could harm someone or themselves.
- Refusing to accept criticism.
- Arguing with your decisions.
- Refusing to accept responsibility for their behavior.
- Lying.
- Not letting you know where they are.

As you can see, a number of these relate directly to some of the aggressive behavior we've been talking about. Corrective Teaching gives parents a structured, flexible plan for dealing with aggression and many other kinds of inappropriate behaviors. Used consistently (meaning whenever misbehavior occurs), Corrective Teaching can help reduce aggression and enable children to learn positive ways to get what they want or settle differences with others.

Using Corrective Teaching

As we said earlier, Corrective Teaching has five steps. When you first start using it, be sure to include all of them. This establishes a structure for teaching and lets your son or daughter know what to expect. As your child begins to understand what you're doing, you may be able to go with only two or three steps. As the teacher, you must decide how best to use this tool; that's where flexibility comes in. How you proceed depends on the age and maturity of the child, how often you teach, how the child responds, and whether his or her behavior starts to change.

Here are the steps for Corrective Teaching, followed by an example of how they can be used:

Step 1. Stop and/or describe the problem behavior.

Step 2. Give a consequence.

Step 3. Describe the behavior the child should use.

Step 4. Give a reason for using the appropriate behavior.

Step 5. Practice the new behavior.

Seven-year-old Jimmy is pushing 8-year-old Latonda because she has a ball he wants.

Step 1. The first step is to tell Jimmy to stop. You must have Jimmy's full attention before you can continue, and you always want to stop any behavior that could hurt someone. It's also very important to specifically describe Jimmy's behavior to him so that he knows what you want him to stop doing. In this situation, you would tell Jimmy that he's pushing Latonda.

Step 2. Once Jimmy is quiet and looking at you, tell him he's earned a consequence for pushing Latonda. Consequences are the results of a person's behavior; they can occur naturally – a skinned knee is the natural consequence of falling down on the sidewalk – or they can be purposely given. In Corrective Teaching, they are purposely given to show children there is a connection between what they do and what happens to them or others.

There are two kinds of consequences – positive and negative. Positive consequences are things a person likes and wants to have or enjoy. They usually are given to reward and encourage appropriate behavior. Negative consequences are things people dislike and want to avoid; they are used to reduce and discourage inappropriate behaviors. Common negative consequences involve having a child do an extra chore or lose a privilege. These kinds of consequences are given in Corrective Teaching.

(Negative consequences should never include acts that physically or emotionally harm a child. Boys Town does not believe in physical punishment like spanking or hitting, and research shows that this kind of response to misbehavior is not effective in helping a child change his or her behaviors.)

In our example, you could have Jimmy go to time-out for 10 minutes. (Time-out is a consequence where a child is removed from the "good stuff," like playing with others, watching TV, or being around you, for a set amount of time.) Always make it clear that the child earned the negative consequence because he or she used a specific behavior.

Step 3. Now describe to Jimmy what he should do the next time he wants something someone else has. This gives him a choice so he doesn't have to respond only with negative behaviors. You could tell Jimmy that he can politely ask for the ball next time or wait until Latonda is done playing with it.

Step 4. The next step – giving a reason for using the new behavior – is a key step in this process. This is where a child learns the benefits of using the behavior. For a younger child like Jimmy, the reasons that mean the most will be those that spell out what good things will happen to him. (This is called a "self-centered" reason.) In this example, a good reason for having Jimmy ask for the ball politely is that Latonda is more likely to give him the ball. When parents have used Corrective Teaching for a while, they can begin giving "other-centered" reasons. These reasons explain how others will benefit when a youth uses an appropriate behavior. Teaching other-centered reasons helps children understand that their behavior can have a positive effect on others, and that it is good to do something for another person. (More on the importance of reasons later.)

Step 5. Finally, practice the new behavior with Jimmy. Practice is what helps the child to learn the new behavior and remember to use it next time. Practice is what eventually "cements" the behavior into a child's routine. Tell Jimmy to pretend that you are Latonda and that you have the ball he wants. Then have Jimmy politely ask you for the ball, the same way he would if he was actually talking to Latonda. If Jimmy forgets what to say or do, start over and have him try it again. If he does a good job, praise him for practicing. Then have him go to time-out for his consequence.

This was a simple example of how to use Corrective Teaching. The consequences and instructions you give might be somewhat different with an older child or a child who is accustomed to your teaching, but the basic structure and steps are the same. Your ability as a parent to use them naturally and consistently will determine how much success you have.

Here's another example, this time with an older youth. We've included all five steps again to demonstrate what the dialogue sounds like.

Mom overhears her 15-year-old son, Nathan, threatening to beat up his younger brother if the boy doesn't give him some money. Mom calls to Nathan and asks him to sit down at the kitchen table.

Step 1. Stop and/or describe the problem behavior.

Mom: "Nathan, just now I heard you telling Bobby that you were going to beat him up if he didn't give you some money. Is that right?"

Nathan: "Yeah, I guess."

Step 2. Give consequence.

Mom: "That kind of behavior is not allowed in our family. For threatening your brother, you are grounded for two days. That means not having anyone over and not going anywhere, except for school. I also want you to apologize to Bobby. Do you understand?"

Nathan: "Yeah."

Step 3. Describe the behavior the child should use.

Mom: "Nathan, what did you need the money for?"

Nathan: "Chet has a new CD. I heard it at his house yesterday and I wanted to buy it. I don't have any money, but I knew Bobby did."

Mom: "Nathan, you know that there are a lot of things you can do around the house to earn money for a CD. The next time you need some money, you should ask me or Dad what chores need to be done and do them."

Nathan: "Okay."

Step 4. Give a reason for using the appropriate behavior.

Mom: "Working around the house is an honest way to earn some money. And it's wrong to scare your brother and make him afraid of you. Do you understand?"

Nathan: "Yes."

Step 5. Practice the new behavior.

Mom: "Let's pretend that you need some money to go to a movie with your friends. What would you do and what would you say?"

Nathan: "I'd come to you or Dad and say, 'Some of the guys are going to a movie but I don't have any money. What can I do around the house to earn some?'"

Mom: "Nice job! Now please go and apologize to your brother."

In this example, Nathan paid attention, cooperated, and accepted his consequences without arguing. But teaching doesn't always go this smoothly.

, your child won't want to listen to you. _ay be angry or upset. When this happens, you will have to decide whether it is better to continue your teaching on the problem behavior or move to another method called Crisis Teaching that shows your child how to calm down and regain self-control. We will discuss how and when to use Crisis Teaching in the next chapter.

Helpful Hints

Your own behaviors while using Corrective Teaching will have a major impact on whether your child pays attention and learns what you are trying to teach. Here are some hints for how to make your teaching compassionate, meaningful, and effective.

Remain calm. Many parents have told us that this one of the most important parts of teaching. They also say it is the most difficult. It's easy to get angry when it seems like you're constantly trying to keep your kids in line. Before that happens, stop, think about what you need to do, calm yourself, and then teach. Some good ways to calm down are slowly counting to 20, taking several deep breaths, or going to another room for a few minutes. Staying calm also can help your child stay calm, and teaching to a calm child is easier than teaching to one who is yelling, pouting, or jumping around.

Be flexible. As your children change, so will your teaching. Continue to use the Corrective Teaching model but feel free to experiment. For instance, if you find that your son responds better and stays calmer when you put the consequence at the end, go with it. No one knows your child better than you. Use Corrective Teaching in the way that best meets what you and your child need.

Remember reasons. We mentioned earlier that giving reasons helps kids understand why they should learn and use positive behaviors. Reasons by themselves don't change behavior, but they can have a big impact when parents use them in their teaching. Kids want to know why they should behave a certain way; they like it when someone gives them a good reason for doing something, and they are more likely to accept reasons that are fair and make sense.

There are two types of reasons: self-centered and other-centered. Reasons that are **self-centered** point out a personal benefit for the youth. For example, a parent might tell his daughter that if she follows an instruction to clean her room right away, she'll have more time to do something she wants to do. This reason is personal and gives the youth an incentive to follow through with the desired behavior.

Self-centered reasons usually work best when parents are just starting to use Corrective Teaching. (The child's age, developmental ability, and personal needs are other factors to consider.) When kids regularly hear reasons for why they should behave a certain way, it helps them better understand the relationship between what they do and what happens to them. As children begin to experience the benefits of using new behaviors, parents can begin to use more other-centered reasons.

Other-centered reasons point out how a youth's behavior may affect others, either positively or negatively. For example, a parent might say: "If you talk softly instead of yelling, you won't bother your sister when she's trying to do her homework" (positive), or "If you steal from a store, you hurt the people who own it. Selling the items is the way they make money to buy food for their families" (negative).

Sometimes, it's a good idea to pair other-centered reasons with self-centered reasons. Here's an example: "If you share your toys with your friends when they come over, they'll have more fun playing with you (other-centered) and they'll want to play with you more often (self-centered)."

Studies have shown that children whose parents use other-centered reasons are more likely to show more mature moral development and less aggression. An offshoot of all this is that children develop a conscience and a value system that helps them learn right from wrong and make healthy choices. As positive behaviors become a permanent part of a child's personality, the child begins to act out of concern for others because it makes him or her feel good and because it is the right thing to do. Eventually, kids treat other people better because they want to, not because someone is making them.

Teach, don't preach. Kids don't like long speeches, especially ones that start with, "When I was your age...." It's best to keep your teaching brief and to the point. A lot of kids, especially younger ones, don't have a long attention span, so it's a good idea to stick to the steps and complete your teaching. Teaching may take longer if you are dealing with a serious behavior, but that's where flexibility comes in. Always be prepared for the unexpected.

Stick to one issue. Believe it or not, kids sometimes don't want to listen to their parents' teaching. They may say things like, "You don't love me," or "My friends' parents are a lot nicer than you" to get you sidetracked off the topic. But stick with what you want to teach. If your child really wants to discuss other issues, tell him or her you will sit down later and talk about them.

Provide a chance for the child to earn back part of a consequence. If your child pays attention, works hard to learn a new behavior, and does well during practice, you can give back part of the consequence. For instance, in our earlier example, Nathan

103

was grounded for two days for threatening his brother. If Nathan did a good job of listening and practicing, and then sincerely apologized to his brother, his mom could give back one day. (A good rule of thumb is to give back up to half of the original consequence.) This is a good way to teach children to make up for their mistakes or misbehaviors, and provides an added incentive to participate and learn new behaviors.

Be consistent. Once you start using Corrective Teaching (and other teaching methods we discuss), it is important to use it whenever an inappropriate behavior occurs. Teaching to some misbehaviors and letting others go will confuse kids and undermine what you are trying to accomplish. When you are consistent, kids begin to understand what you expect of them. This improves their cooperation and makes teaching more pleasant and effective in the long run.

Use consequences and follow through. It may be difficult sometimes to give your child consequences for misbehavior. You may even feel guilty about it. But remember that children must learn that there is a connection between what they do and what happens to them. This will be true all of their lives. Consequences help children make that connection and understand that their behavior affects them and others.

As we said earlier, negative consequences usually involve taking away a privilege or adding an extra chore. Taking away a privilege could mean grounding your child, having him or her go to time-out, or losing TV time. Extra chores could include vacuuming, cleaning the bathroom, washing the car, helping a brother or sister with a chore, mowing the lawn, or cleaning the garage.

Don't be afraid to give consequences and follow through with them. Your kids may not like getting consequences at first, especially if you haven't given them in the past. But consistently teaching and using consequences will eventually bring about the positive changes you want to see in your kids' behavior.

Neither Corrective Teaching nor any of the teaching methods we offer in this book are miracle "cures" for aggression. They are only tools that give parents something to work with as they try to prevent or reduce aggressive or violent behavior in their children. Becoming a better teacher will help you become a better parent. But teaching must be done with sincerity and love. Children know when you're just going through the motions; they have to know that you are genuinely concerned about them for the teaching you do to work. As you read the next chapters, remember that teaching does not occur in a vacuum; it happens within the relationship you have with your kids. The stronger that relationship is, the more effective your teaching will be.

CHAPTER 12

When Children Lose Control

Dad asks Donita to take some clothes out of the dryer and fold them. Donita, who is watching TV, ignores him. In a little louder voice, Dad again asks Donita to help. Donita yells, "Can't you see I'm watching my show? I always have to do all the d---- chores." Dad sighs and walks away, and Donita goes back to her program.

Mom tells Jason that he has to hurry or he'll be late for school. Jason responds, "Would you get off my back? The h--- with school. I don't care if I'm late." This makes Mom mad and she yells, "Don't you dare talk to me that way. Get moving right now!" Jason raises his fist and screams, *"Leave me alone! You can't tell me what to do!"* Mom threatens to ground Jason for two weeks if he doesn't *"shut his big mouth."* Now Jason steps toward his mom and hollers, *"You better back off right now and get the h--- away from me!"* Mom gives up and retreats to the kitchen.

Eight-year-old Samuel is watching television when his older brother, Carlos, walks up and grabs the remote control from him. Samuel yells and jumps up, and Carlos punches him in the shoulder several times. Mom hears all this from the kitchen and stomps into the living room. By this time, both boys are hitting each other and wrestling on the floor. Mom begins screaming that she's had it with their fighting over the TV. When the boys ignore her and continue to fight, she separates them, slaps each on the arm, and goes back to the kitchen. Carlos, who still has the remote control, plops onto the couch, sticks his tongue out at Samuel, and changes the channel.

You've just read three examples of what can happen when a parent has had little success in stopping his or her child's aggressive behavior. In the first one, Dad decided to escape as soon as Donita shouted at him. To Dad, her yelling was a "punishing" act, and it was easier and less painful for him to get away from it rather than to confront it. In the second example, Mom and Jason took turns trying to top each other with negative behaviors until one of them finally backed down. Jason won the battle when he threatened his mom. In the final example, Mom lashed out at Samuel and Carlos, first yelling at them about fighting, then slapping the boys. She may have stopped the fight, but she didn't give any consequences or teach the boys a positive way to settle their differences. And Carlos, who started the fight, was rewarded for his aggressive behavior because he got to keep the remote control he took from his brother.

If these are the wrong ways to respond to serious misbehaviors, what is the right way? You could try Corrective Teaching. And in some situations, it might work. But if a child is angry and uncooperative, and beyond the point of following instructions or paying attention to what you're saying, you might not get very far. This is especially true with an aggressive child. Usually, when behaviors like yelling, swearing, hitting, throwing things, or stubbornly refusing to follow instructions continue as you try to teach, it signals a crisis. When this happens, you must go a step beyond Corrective Teaching to a special method called **Crisis Teaching**.

Crisis Teaching can help parents accomplish two goals. First, it provides parents with a way to calm a child and defuse what is often a very emotional situation. It is impossible to teach a child who has lost self-control and is not able to make good choices about what behaviors to use. Crisis Teaching allows the child and the parent time to retreat, settle down, and come back together in a more positive and less emotional frame of mind. The second goal is to teach children how to make good choices on their own when they get upset. Parents and other responsible adults are not always going to be around when children find themselves in situations where things aren't going well. Crisis Teaching helps kids learn how to identify and express their feelings in a calm, appropriate manner in almost any situation, a skill that is necessary at home, in school, on the playground, and in the workplace. Whether you are trying to prevent aggression or correct aggressive behaviors, Crisis Teaching gives you a structured plan for responding when your child refuses to listen to you and follow instructions, or "blows up" and completely loses self-control.

Discipline is the art of teaching children self-control using consequences.[1] When kids learn to make good decisions about their behavior on their own and can exercise that kind of control in many social settings, everyone wins.

The Steps of Crisis Teaching

Crisis Teaching is more complicated than Corrective Teaching because it usually occurs in situations like the ones we've just described – a child is upset and uncooperative, his or her behavior is disrupting the teaching you are trying to do, and you're struggling to control your own highly charged behavior. As parents, we know what it's like to have a child talk back, slam doors, scream, cry, hit, kick, or behave in other ways we don't like. It makes us angry, hurts our feelings, and makes us dislike our kids. We want the behavior to stop immediately, and we know that yelling and lashing out can accomplish that goal. But that's not what teaching and good parenting are about. Teaching is about helping kids control their behaviors over the long run by giving them positive behaviors to use in place of negative behaviors. Good parenting is about doing this teaching with love and genuine concern in a positive manner.

The point here is that effective teaching is impossible when both the parent and the child are upset. That's why Crisis Teaching is divided into two parts. The first part focuses on stopping the misbehavior and giving everyone involved an opportunity to calm down. This helps reduce or remove a lot of the negative emotions that can make teaching difficult in these situations. Once the misbehavior has stopped and the child is calm, parents can move to the second part of Crisis Teaching. This is where a child learns ways to maintain self-control, practices them, and receives a consequence for the original misbehavior.

Like Corrective Teaching, Crisis Teaching offers both structure and flexibility. Each step is designed to help you accomplish a specific teaching goal. When you first start using Crisis Teaching, you should include all the steps; later, as your child becomes more responsive to your teaching, you can choose the steps that you think are necessary in particular situations. The steps also can be modified and used in different combinations. It comes down to what works best for you and your children. Crisis Teaching is a parenting tool, so how you use it with your children will determine how well it works.

The next section identifies and describes each step of Crisis Teaching. This may seem like a lot to remember, especially during the "heat of battle." Usually, though, if you can focus on the two main parts, Calming Down and Follow-Up Teaching, the steps themselves are easier to remember and follow in a logical order. Once you've memorized these steps, it will be easier to concentrate on your child's behaviors and teach rather than allowing yourself to get drawn into an argument or a fight.

Part One: Calming Down

Step 1. Stop the problem behavior.

Step 2. Describe the problem behavior.

Step 3. Give clear instructions.

Step 4. Allow time to calm down.

Part Two: Follow-Up Teaching

Step 5. Describe what your child can do differently next time.

Step 6. Give a reason for using the new behavior.

Step 7. Practice what your child can do next time.

Step 8. Give a consequence.

Part One: Calming Down

Step 1. Stop the problem behavior.

In many situations, a firm instruction can stop a child's verbal misbehavior (yelling, screaming, cussing, crying, etc.). (If this happens, you may be able to do Corrective Teaching instead of Crisis Teaching.) If a child does not stop the behavior, he or she should be allowed to calm down and the instruction should be given again. (Don't keep repeating the instruction over and over; this comes across as nagging and may make the situation worse.)

Any physical behavior that could harm the child or others should be stopped immediately. You can first tell the child to stop, but if the behavior is serious and dangerous (punching, kicking, hitting someone with an object, etc.), you should act quickly and use only as much physical force as necessary. This might involve putting a hand on a child's shoulder, separating two or more children who are wrestling or fighting, taking hold of the arms of a child who is hitting the parent or someone else, firmly "bear-hugging" a child who is swinging his fists or kicking wildly, or taking away an object that is being used as a weapon. Continuing to give a firm command for the child to stop also can be helpful.

A parent should never hit or kick a child, throw a child to the floor or against a wall or furniture, use any kind of object to poke or hit a child, twist a child's arm or leg, or do anything else abusive that could hurt the child.

So if you see your son Tommy punching Janie, the first thing you would do is separate the two and check to make sure Janie is okay. Then you could tell your son, "Stop hitting Janie now. We don't allow hitting in our house." This tells him that you are serious and that his behavior is not acceptable.

Step 2. Describe the problem behavior.

This is a step where saying a little is better than saying a lot. A child who is upset doesn't want to hear you go on and on about what he or she is doing wrong. So, speaking slowly and in a calm voice, briefly and clearly describe your child's negative behavior. (Don't try to "talk over" what your child might be saying; wait for breaks.) Use words your child understands, and be as specific as possible. At this point, your child only needs to know what he or she is doing. In our example where Tommy was punching Janie, you could say, "Tommy, while I was standing here, I saw you hit Janie in the arm with your fist."

Most importantly, stay calm and don't let anger or sarcasm creep into what you are saying. Also, avoid judgmental or hurtful comments like, "Stop acting like a baby" or "That's a really stupid thing to do." This only adds fuel to the fire and makes matters worse. Sometimes it is very difficult not to get mad, especially when your child is doing something that drives you crazy. But just as in any other teaching, staying calm is the key to success.

It's also a good idea during this step to show your child that you care about how he or she feels. Telling your child that you understand that he or she is upset can have a calming effect, start your teaching on a positive note, and help you focus on the child's behavior rather than your own emotions.

Step 3. Give clear instructions.

This step also should be kept short and to the point. Its purpose is to tell your child exactly what he or she should do to start calming down. For example, you can tell your child to go to his or her room, ask the child to sit on the couch and take a few deep breaths, or have the child slowly count to 20. Whatever instructions you give, don't keep repeating them if the child doesn't do what you ask. Give only one or two instructions so he or she doesn't become confused. If a child absolutely refuses to listen to you or follow instructions, go on to the next step.

Step 4. Allow time to calm down.

In an emotional, stressful situation like Crisis Teaching, time spent away from your child is sometimes just as important as the time you spend together. Time is your ally here; it gives both you and your child a chance to put emotions aside and focus on the teaching that's coming up. It's like a time-out in a sports contest; the action stops and the players go to the sidelines to plan strategy and decide what to do next. For you and your child, the "sidelines" might be a quiet place where you both can be alone for a while.

When everyone calms down, it's easier to complete the next three steps, and your child is more likely to listen and follow instructions. Your child probably won't be happy, but he or she should be able to talk to you without losing self-control again.

Take as much time as you need. You can periodically check with your child to see if he or she is ready to talk to you. (Once you've used Crisis Teaching a few times, you can tell your child during these checks that the more times you have to come back, the larger the consequence will be for the misbehavior. This sometimes motivates kids to calm down quickly.) When your child can answer your questions calmly and appears ready to cooperate, go to the next step.

Part Two: Follow-Up Teaching

Step 5. Describe what your child can do differently next time.

Here's where kids start to learn how to handle frustration, anger, and other negative feelings in appropriate ways. One of the best ways to teach this skill is by using the "instead of..." phrase. It goes like this:

"Instead of swearing when you get angry, please tell me you're mad and ask if you can go to your room and calm down."

"Instead of kicking the wall when you can't do something, tell me that you're frustrated and ask if you can take a break."

At Boys Town, we have developed a number of "self-control strategies" that parents can teach their kids. A child who learns two or three of these strategies and gets good at using them is more likely to respond to upsetting situations in a calm and positive manner. Here are the strategies and how to use them:

Deep-breathing

- Silently count to five as you take a deep breath in through your nose.
- Hold the breath for five seconds.
- Count to five again as you let the breath out slowly through your mouth.
- Take two normal breaths.
- Repeat the first four steps two or three times until you feel yourself calming down.
- When you are calm, tell an adult.

Writing or drawing in a journal

- Go someplace where you won't be disturbed.
- Write down (or draw a picture that shows) how you are feeling and what you are thinking.
- When you are calm, tell an adult.

Take time to cool down

- Go some place where you won't be disturbed or distracted.
- Take five minutes to calm down.
- If you need more time, calmly ask for it.
- When you are calm, tell an adult.

Positive self-talk

- Make a positive comment about how you can handle a situation appropriately. Use a phrase like, "I can get myself under control"; "I've done it before, I can do it again"; "If I stop now, things will get better"; or "I can do this."
- Repeat the statement you choose until you are calm.
- When you are calm, tell an adult.

Muscle relaxation

- Clench and squeeze your fists for five seconds and slowly release them.
- Slowly roll your neck in circles for five seconds.
- Scrunch your shoulders and slowly roll them in circles several times.
- Slowly rotate your ankles.
- Raise your eyebrows as high as you can and slowly lower them.
- Scrunch your face and release.
- When you are calm, tell an adult.

Another important part of this step is helping children recognize what makes them upset and what happens when they start to feel that way. For example, if you notice that your son always gets angry when someone teases him, and that he starts breathing faster just before he blows up, you can explain this to your son when you reach this step in Crisis Teaching. (You also could do this as part of Proactive Teaching, described in Chapter 8.) Then you can teach him a self-control strategy, such as asking to go to his room to calm down, that he can use instead. Eventually, your son will learn to recognize the situation (teasing) and the signal (breathing faster), and know that he can choose an appropriate way to respond.

Be patient; change won't take place overnight. It takes time for kids to unlearn negative behaviors and learn new positive behaviors. But when they do, it makes a world of difference in how they express their feelings, control their behaviors, and get along with others.

Step 6. Give a reason for using the new behavior.

Just as in Corrective Teaching, this is where a parent tells a child why he or she should use the appropriate behavior that is being taught. When you first start teaching or are teaching to a younger child, start with self-centered reasons, those that tell the child what he or she will get out of using the new behavior. (For example, you can tell Tommy that if he doesn't hit people, he won't get in trouble.) Later, begin giving other-centered reasons that explain how others will benefit from the child's positive behavior.

(An other-centered reason for Tommy would be that when he decides not to hit, other people don't get hurt.) As mentioned earlier, the goal is to have children choose positive behaviors because they understand that it is the right thing to do.

Step 7. Practice what your child can do next time.

Because it can be very difficult for children and youth to learn how to keep their emotions and behaviors in check in certain situations, practice is vitally important to the teaching and learning process. Having kids practice prepares them to make good choices about their behavior the next time they get angry or upset.

Practice also allows you and your child to work together. Children are much more likely to want to learn if they understand that their parents do what they do out of love and concern. And practice can be fun. Making up situations and playing the parts of the people involved is a great way to reduce a child's anxiety and make learning enjoyable. For example, your daughter may get a kick out of "switching places" with you, so that you pretend to be her and she pretends to be you. How you portray her may give her a better idea of how she looks, how she acts, and what she says when she's upset. That may motivate her to improve how she handles those situations in the future.

Some kids may be afraid to try something new because they think they'll fail or be embarrassed. This can be a major obstacle to learning. Practice helps kids overcome this fear by giving them an opportunity to try new strategies and make mistakes without having to worry about failure. In fact, parents can reward their kids for good practices, which motivates kids to try harder. So kids actually have a chance to succeed without the risk of failing.

Step 8. Give a consequence.

It's not unusual for parents to want to skip or forget this step when they do Crisis Teaching. The negative behavior has stopped, the child is calm, and he or she just did a great job of practicing a self-control strategy. Why would you want to give a negative consequence and risk upsetting the child again?

The answer is that consequences help change behavior. Giving a negative consequence every time a child loses self-control is necessary to show kids the connection between what they do and what happens to them. Following through with that consequence lets kids know that you are serious about helping them change their behaviors. They begin to understand that you won't let misbehaviors slip by and that they have to pay a price for losing self-control. Over time, angry outbursts diminish and children learn how to control their emotions and behaviors.

If possible, tie the consequence to the misbehavior. So if your child gets mad and slams his bicycle down, complete your teaching and take away the bicycle for a while.

Using Crisis Teaching

The following example will give you an idea of what Crisis Teaching sounds like.

Thirteen-year-old Tyler comes home from school upset over a low grade he received on a book report. When Tyler goes into the kitchen, his mom and his younger brother, James, are sitting at the table. James says, "Tyler, I got an 'A' on my spelling test today." Tyler slams his bookbag on the table and replies, "Why don't you shut up. I don't care what you got on your spelling test. You're just a suck-up mama's boy."

Mom asks Tyler what's wrong. Tyler starts yelling about how his teacher is "stupid" and unfair because she gave him a 'C' on his report. When Mom tries to start doing Corrective Teaching for what Tyler said to his brother, Tyler continues to shout and then lunges toward James and kicks him in the leg. Mom immediately steps between the boys, takes Tyler by the arm, and guides him to a chair on the other side of the kitchen. She tells Tyler, who is still yelling, to sit in the chair, then goes over to check on James.

When she sees James is okay, she asks him to go to the basement and watch TV so she can talk to Tyler, who now is shouting and kicking his chair with his heels. James leaves the kitchen, and Mom starts Crisis Teaching.

Part 1: Calming Down

Step 1. Stop the problem behavior.

Mom: "I know you're upset over the grade you got on your report, but please stop yelling and kicking the chair." (Mom has already stopped the problem behavior of Tyler kicking James.)

Tyler stops kicking the chair, but continues to yell that James always gets treated better.

Step 2. Describe the problem behavior.

Mom: "Thanks for not kicking the chair anymore. You're still shouting."

(When Tyler stops shouting for a few seconds, Mom continues.) *"Before, when you came into the kitchen, you yelled at your brother and called him a name. You also kicked him in the leg. You know that none of that is allowed in our home."*

Step 3. Give clear instructions.

Mom: "Tyler, why don't you go to your room and calm down. I'll check on you in a few minutes to see if you're ready to talk about this."

Tyler goes to his room and closes the door.

Step 4. Allow time to calm down.

After five minutes, Mom goes to Tyler's room and knocks on the door.

Mom: "Tyler, are you ready to talk with me about what happened when you came home?"

Tyler (in a calm voice): "You can come in."

Part II: Follow-Up Teaching

Step 5. Describe what your child can do differently next time.

Mom: "Tyler, let's talk about what you can do the next time you're upset over a grade."

Tyler: "James is always bragging about how good he does in school."

Mom: "Tyler, we're not talking about James right now. Please don't interrupt me. I know it's not always easy to accept how a teacher grades your papers, but when you get upset over it, I'd like you to ask me if you can go to your room and calm down. Once you're calm, we can discuss the grade."

Step 6. Give a reason for using the new behavior.

Mom: "If you go to your room and calm down when you're upset, you're less likely to get mad at your

125

brother and kick him. Then he won't get hurt and you won't get a consequence. You know that we don't allow hitting or kicking. When you're calm, I'll be glad to sit down with you and go over your paper."

Step 7. Practice what your child can do next time.

Mom: "Let's practice what you can do the next time you're upset over something. Let's pretend that you just got home from school and you're upset because you've got a ton of homework and you won't be able to play football after school. Tell me what you would say."

Tyler: "Mom, I'm kinda mad because I've got a lot of homework. Can I go to my room and calm down?"

Mom: "Tyler, that was great. You asked to go to your room, and you looked at me and used a nice voice. That's exactly what you should do whenever you're upset."

Step 8. Give a consequence.

Mom: "We do have consequences for yelling at and kicking other people. So you've lost television for two nights. I'd also like you to go apologize to your brother. When you're done, bring your report back here and we'll go over it together."

Helpful Hints

All of the suggestions offered in Chapter 11 for Corrective Teaching apply to Crisis Teaching. Here are a few more that can help make Crisis Teaching more effective.

Stay calm. We've mentioned this before, but it's so important that it bears repeating. Your ability to stay calm will determine whether Crisis Teaching works. If your child is angry or upset and you get angry or upset, the only thing that will happen is an argument. It is vital that you train yourself not to let anything your child says or does make you lose self-control or become angry. Remaining relaxed and calm also models the behaviors you want your child to use and lets the child know that you are serious about teaching him or her new behaviors.

There are several ways to show that you are calm. First, you can talk slower and softer. Sometimes, this will cause your child to lower his or her voice. You also can continue to tell your child that you understand that he or she is upset. Statements like, "I know you're having a hard time right now," or "It's not easy to have to deal with a problem like this," show that you are concerned and are going to hang in there to help the child get through a difficult time. Don't forget to notice and praise improvements in your child's behavior, no matter how small they might be. If your child is turned away from you and then follows your instruction to look at you, say, "Great! Thanks for facing me. That's much better."

Finally, stick to the issue at hand. Children will sometimes try to change the subject so they can get out of trouble or make you leave them alone. They might even make accusations and nasty comments like, "You are so unfair"; "You always treat me worse than the other kids"; "You're a lousy parent and I hate you"; or "You don't really love me." As we've mentioned before, don't get sidetracked. Either ignore what the child is saying or tell him or her that you'll discuss other matters later. Right now, it's time to deal with the child's behavior.

We've already said that situations where Crisis Teaching is necessary are highly emotional. Usually, your child will supply enough emotion for the both of you. Don't waste your energy and lose your focus by trying to match your child angry word for angry word or aggressive behavior for aggressive behavior. It will only make matters worse and take away from what otherwise can be a positive teaching opportunity.

Pick your battles. Sometimes, parents overreact to their children's behaviors and jump into Crisis Teaching too quickly. If this happens a lot, a child might start thinking that his or her parents are going to make a federal case out of even the most minor misbehavior. This is not a healthy situation for children or parents. It's usually best to consider whether Corrective Teaching will do the job when a misbehavior occurs. If the negative behavior continues or is so extreme that you have no other choice, then start Crisis Teaching.

There also will be times when teaching is not the answer. Sometimes, kids get so overwhelmed or confused by their emotions that they just need someone to listen. Simply asking a child if there's a problem and telling him or her that you're there to help can sometimes prevent or calm a potentially volatile situation. For example, say something like, "I know you're upset. If you can calm down, we can talk about it." You know your kids better than anyone. The more you teach and the more your child learns, the easier it should be for you to decide whether to use Crisis Teaching or some other intervention.

Be aware of your physical actions. While teaching, your physical actions are as important as what you say and how you say it. Using behaviors that your child might interpret as being aggressive or threatening may only serve to make a bad situation even worse. These behaviors might include "stalking" or shadowing your child if he or she leaves the room, using a harsh or demanding voice, standing over a child to establish your "dominance," pointing your index finger, standing with your hands on your hips, raising a fist, or putting your face close to the child's face; all of these gestures set the stage for confrontation rather than conversation.

Parents have told us that sitting down, being at eye level with a child, keeping their hands in their pockets, or folding their arms over their chests helps them avoid these gestures and others that might seem intimidating to a child. Another calming method that works is the deep-breathing exercise that was described earlier.

Plan consequences ahead of time. When kids know the consequences for negative behavior, they are more aware of the connection between their behavior and what happens to them. A good idea might be to have your kids help you come up with appropriate consequences for misbehaviors; your kids will see you as being fair and they will feel like they have a say in the teaching process. Also, having planned consequences helps avoid situations where you might hand out unreasonable or harsh punishment because you are angry.

Try to set up "happy" endings. In this case, a "happy" ending refers to wrapping up Crisis Teaching in such a way that the matter is settled and both the parent and child walk away without hating each other. Children may not always be happy with the way things turn out; in fact, there may be times when they aren't happy at all. But unhappiness over what happens should not translate to disrespect or dislike. Children must understand that you do what you do out of love, and that even though you don't like how they choose to behave, you still love them as people.

Some endings may call for a problem-solving approach where you help your child find solutions for situations that cause trouble. Other times, Crisis Teaching can end with a firm, matter-of-fact statement. (In the example with Tyler, Mom told him to apologize to his brother, then get his report so they could go over it.) Sometimes, kids cry after an especially intense teaching session because they just don't know how to express what they're feeling. That's when parents need to show compassion and understanding, and ask the child why he or she feels so angry or so sad or so frustrated. Talking with your child and allowing him or her to release pent-up emotions shows that you care, and can provide some valuable insight into why certain behaviors are occurring.

Talk about why it's harmful to use aggressive behaviors. Sometimes, parents assume that their kids know all the negative results of using aggressive behaviors. That's not true. Oftentimes, children act without thinking, then are surprised when they have to pay the price later. When kids realize that many bad things can happen to them when they rely on aggression to solve problems or get what they want, they might be less likely to behave aggressively. For example, parents can explain to their kids that using aggressive behaviors can cause them to lose friends, have trouble in school, run into hassles with adults, get arrested, get a reputation as a bully, or be left out of enjoyable activities. Children must understand that these are not acceptable outcomes, and that they can avoid them by getting along with others and solving problems in positive ways.

Be patient. Wise parents know that learning self-control can take a long time. So don't expect too much too soon, and don't be disappointed when your kids don't show improvement as quickly as you'd like. Pay attention to small victories, and heap praise on your child for even the smallest bit of progress. Above all, don't give up. The stakes for your children, and for you, are much too high.

In our earlier example, Tyler did what his mom asked and calmed down fairly quickly. In real-life, kids don't always cooperate so easily. Some kids can continue their misbehavior for a long time, or calm down for a while and then lose self-control again. You also may have to deal with other distractions while you're teaching. Above all, remain calm and keep the situation under control. This is some of the most important teaching you will do, whether you are dealing with or trying to prevent aggressive or violent behavior.

When you first start using Crisis Teaching (or any of the Boys Town teaching methods), your teaching might seem somewhat rigid and stilted. It also may be hard to remember all the steps and what you can say with each one. That's natural. But it is very important to establish a structure for your teaching. This helps your child become familiar with the process and your expectations. Over time, as you develop your own personal style, your teaching will become more natural and conversational. This kind of teaching is most effective in helping your children learn new skills.

Dealing with a child who is upset is a difficult task. Crisis Teaching may not always make it easier, but it does give you a plan for helping your child calm down, get back on track, and eventually learn ways to maintain self-control on his or her own in many different situations.

So far in this book, we have talked about the many effective ways you can confront and change aggressive (and other negative) behaviors in your child. Now we're going to throw you a curve. None of these methods work very well – unless you have a strong relationship with your child.

Relationships between parents and their children should be built on mutual respect, trust, caring, sharing, loving, and closeness. The bond between parents and their children should be flexible and yielding, but unbreakable. In other words, as kids grow and develop, and their parents let them enjoy more independence and freedom, the bond can stretch but never break. The strength of this bond is tested every time a parent has to discipline his or her child. But if kids understand that parents act out of love and concern, the lessons being taught begin to make sense and take hold. Your children must know that you love them unconditionally and that you will always be there for them.

In the next two chapters, we will talk about what parents and kids can do to build stronger relationships and how raising the level of love in families can lower the level of aggressive behavior.

---

[1] Cloud, H., & Townsend, J. (1992). **Boundaries**. Grand Rapids, MI: Zondervan Publishing House.

Build Strong
Relationships

CHAPTER 13

Talk, Listen, and Love

There is more to parenting than telling children
what they should and should not do. Parenting is
a commitment to loving a child unconditionally, acting with warmth and concern no matter what happens. This is at the heart of a strong, loving relationship between a parent and a child.

Your relationship with your child began the day
he or she was born. That new baby was totally
dependent on you for food, clothing, baths, clean dia-
pers, medicine, and all the other physical necessities
of life. But as important as those are, you provided
something else whose value cannot be measured.
Babies can't comprehend what love is, but that little
person knew your face, your embrace, and your
voice. Whether you were toting your baby around the
house, standing over the crib making funny faces, or

changing a diaper for the tenth time that day, your child felt safe and secure just because he or she knew you were there. And that made you feel good.

Obviously, children change as they get older and so do parents. Relationships change, too. But the bond between a child and a parent must remain constant. So ask yourself this question: Do my kids still know I'm there for them, and does that still make me feel good? How you answer will give you a good idea about whether you have a strong, loving relationship with your children.

As children get older, their relationships with their parents will constantly be tested. Unless you have a perfect child (nobody does) or are a perfect parent (nobody is), there will be times when disagreements cause tension, anxiety, anger, frustration, and other negative feelings. Your kids will assert their independence, and you will assert your parental authority. Peer pressure and the need to fit in will sometimes be more powerful than the influence you have on your child's life. This is a normal part of growing up. But strong, trusting relationships survive. That's the payoff for creating and nurturing a bond with your child that can withstand any challenge over the years.

One way to know whether you are succeeding is to measure how often you and your kids talk with each other about what's happening in your lives. These are conversations that go far beyond the parent's question, "How's school going?" and the child's response of "Fine." Meaningful communication is a key to healthy relationships; when two people share their feelings, thoughts, fears, and ideas, there is more trust and respect and fewer misunderstandings that can lead to problems. (More on this later.) Kids might never admit it, but most believe their parents are the best sounding board they have as they grow and begin to find their place in the world. If your kids trust you with their innermost thoughts, it's a good sign that they value and respect your opinion. That's one of the highest compliments you can receive as a parent.

The time to worry is when your kids don't or won't talk to you, and minor disagreements turn into destructive or dangerous battles. Many times, this is where a child's negative and aggressive behaviors start. Relationships suffer in these situations, and in the worst cases, children and parents drift apart and the gap becomes too wide to bridge. This is especially true with older kids.

When good communication is missing in a family, kids also start ignoring their parents and relying on sources outside the home for information they need. For example, a 1998 Time/CNN poll sought to find out where kids learned about sex. Forty-five percent of the respondents cited friends as their main source and 29 percent cited television. Parents ranked third at 7 percent, followed by sex education classes at 3 percent. The danger here is that parental influence can be overshadowed or overwhelmed by outside forces that often provide inaccurate information or send the wrong messages on important issues.

Obviously, there are certain truths, values, and ideas that you want your child to adapt and follow. But you can't force your opinions on your kids or expect them to think like you think. In fact, using that strategy will probably drive them away rather than bring them closer. Instead, treat your kids as individuals who can think for themselves and accomplish goals on their own. This gives kids confidence and lets them know that you trust them.

Our kids are the most important people in our lives. We want what's best for them, and how and what we teach them as children has a lasting and profound effect on their lives. But everything we do must happen within a bond of love that we create and nurture. Parents must teach correct behavior and give consequences, but they also must love.

The remainder of this book will offer a number of ways parents can improve on the relationships they have with their children. It is by no means an all-inclusive list, and you probably can come up with many more that fit your family's situation. As you read them, keep in mind that good parenting involves just the right balance of authority, discipline, teaching, and love. You are a good parent. We hope what we provide here helps make you even better.

Understand that your child sees the world differently. Your kids don't have the same life experiences as you, so how could they possibly view the world the same way? While it's true that we help shape our kids' perceptions, they still have their own feelings and opinions about what happens to them or goes on around them.

Every child is unique in personality, feelings, likes, and dislikes. How children express themselves defines their perception of life and where they fit in. So don't be shocked or surprised when your children say something that doesn't make sense in your "adult" world. It's just a translation of a situation or an issue through a child's eyes.

There will be many times when you and your child won't see eye to eye, especially when it comes to issues like dating, curfew, owning a car, friends, and responsibility. Try to work things out by letting your child know that his or her opinion matters and by listening with an open mind. This doesn't mean that you automatically give in or bend the rules whenever your child wants something or disagrees with you. It does mean that you respect your child's views and consider them when you make a decision. This will make it easier to resolve disagreements before they erupt into arguments and will show your kids that you are fair.

Teach your child how to be a good person. The word "good" can have many definitions when used in describing a person. Generally, however, a good person is someone who lives by a code of high morals and values, treats others with respect, is charitable and forgiving, looks for goodness in others, and always tries to do the right thing.

How do you teach these traits? First, you have to model them, especially in the way you treat other people. Your children are always watching you. They follow your lead and mimic your words and actions. Have you ever watched a little girl play house with her dolls? She will talk to her "kids" in much the same way her mom talks to her and her siblings. Modeling is a powerful and natural way to teach positive behaviors.

Second, start explaining the difference between right and wrong to your children when they are young. It's never too early to start helping your kids build a strong moral foundation. Always be alert for opportunities to point out and discuss good and bad behavior, whether it happens in real life, in a television program or movie, or in a story. Passing along positive morals and values is one of the best gifts you can give your kids, and they will appreciate your efforts.

Don't assume that children simply "know" how to be good. Children are not programmed with positive behaviors at birth, and they don't automatically display them. As we've said so many times, kids learn behaviors. And their primary teachers are their parents.

Be involved in your kids' lives. Show interest in their activities, friends, hobbies, clothing, music, sports, TV shows, movies, etc. Pay particular attention to their schoolwork, and try to stay on top of what's going on in their schools and classrooms. (Going to school open houses and faithfully attending conferences with teachers are musts.) Also, don't miss your child's piano recitals, school or church programs, science fairs, band concerts, dances, ball games, etc.

Sometimes, it's a good idea to be an inactive observer. Sit nearby and listen as your child reads a book or hang out while your child plays with friends on the swing set. Just having you around means a lot to your kids.

As kids get older, they may shun or be embarrassed by your efforts to be involved in their lives. They may even accuse you of interfering or meddling. This is normal, and it usually starts right around the junior high school years. Kids need room to grow and express their independence, and that need can easily run head on into what a parent thinks a child should do. When this happens, it's a good idea to back off a bit but continue to show support and interest. You might not be able to be as involved in activities as you were before (your 17-year-old might feel a little skittish about you going on a date with him or her), but you can continue to ensure your child that what happens in his or her life is important to you.

Finally, avoid "benign neglect." This is a situation where parents equate love with giving their children "stuff" – money, nice stereos, expensive clothes and shoes, cars, etc. What some parents don't realize is that heaping material possessions onto kids does not take the place of spending time together and simply being there every day to meet their emotional needs. Kids need to know their parents care, and that happens only when parents commit themselves to playing an active role in the lives of their children.

Remember: The time you miss with your kids can never be replaced. There are a lot of things you can put off until tomorrow, but spending time with your kids shouldn't be one of them.

Talk with your kids. Conversation is the cornerstone of strong relationships in a family. The problem is that many parents don't use it enough. Research shows that mothers spend about 11 minutes a weekday in conversation with their kids; for fathers, the time is about eight minutes. Even mothers who don't work spend only about 30 minutes talking with their children.

Talking is the main way parents and children communicate. It's how most of the teaching and learning that takes place in a family occurs. Topics of conversation may range from trivial to profound; it doesn't matter. What matters is that parents and their kids are sharing information about themselves and what's going on in their lives. Human beings need to feel like they belong, like they are connected to the people who are closest to them. Talking to someone fulfills that need. And families with strong communication skills are better able to solve problems, make decisions, and get along.

If you and your kids can comfortably talk to each other, you have a great gift; don't lose it. If you have trouble getting conversations started, or you don't know what to talk about, don't worry. Start slowly and work on getting better as you go along.

There are many ways to establish good communication with your kids. Make it clear to them that they can talk to you anytime, not just when they have a problem or need something. Kids are more likely to want to talk with you when they see that you are open and willing to talk. You also can communicate with your kids in other ways, even when you're not around. For instance, leave notes to your kids from time to time. You can use a note to praise a child, share information, or just say that you'll talk later. (If your child did something really great, leave a candy bar or a pack of gum with the note.) Or call your kids on the phone once in a while. They like knowing that you care enough to take the time during a busy day just to see how they're doing.

There should be no shortage of conversation topics when it comes to talking to your kids. Make a point of asking them about their day. Ask about school, their friends, sports, work, church, and activities. Talk about what's going on in the world. Watch the news together and discuss issues.

Talk about funny or silly things that have happened to you, or tell your kids what it was like growing up when you were young. This is a great time to let them know that you've made mistakes and that you don't expect them to be perfect. Many parents react strongly to their kids' misbehaviors or shortcomings because these are exactly the same problems the parents are experiencing or have experienced. Talking about these issues with your kids can be a good way of clearing up misunderstandings or smoothing out hard feelings.

You also can gather up all your old family pictures and have the kids help you put them in a photo album; this is a great way to talk about your family history and relatives. Or have the kids help you arrange all their baby pictures in a special photo album. Kids are naturally curious, so oftentimes it's just a matter of hitting on a topic that they are interested in or wonder about. The more you learn about their interests, the more you will have to talk about.

There will be times when you feel like your kids aren't listening to you or appear to be openly resisting or disagreeing with what you say. Some parents just give up, even if the point they're trying to make is important. But if you know what you are saying is right, or moral, or reasonable, the best thing to do is say it anyway. Kids need time to let things "sink in"; it's better to say what's on your mind and give them something to think about rather than let an opportunity pass by.

How you talk with your kids also is important. Keep in mind that there are different levels of conversation. The way you talk about a child's problems is different from how you talk about the weather. Sometimes, you'll talk to your kids to help them overcome their fears or give them advice; those conversations will be different from ones about their plans for the weekend. There should be a good mix of these levels; not all of your adult-child conversations should be trivial, nor should they all be super serious. But no matter what the topic, conversations between you and your kids are significant "events" that bring you closer together. Each person shares something special about himself or herself; over time, this leads to a deeper connection between moms and dads and sons and daughters.

It's a good idea sometimes to choose when and where you talk with your kids. Of course there will be times when you and your child enjoy a casual conversation, like when you're watching a TV show together or riding in the car. But some issues require a quiet place and a quiet time. A hectic morning, when the kids are trying to get ready for school and you're hustling to get to work on time, probably is not the best time for a serious talk about dating or sex. So take advantage of quiet times during the day or evening when you can give your child your full attention. This is especially true for kids who are using aggressive behaviors. When those behaviors occur, it's time for teaching. If the incident is particularly serious, neither the parent or child may feel like talking about anything afterwards. But a parent can wait for a quiet time later when he or she can talk with the child about other matters. In other words, always be on the lookout for opportunities to reach out and connect with your child.

Think about conversations you've had with your kids over the past few days. Did they involve serious matters or trivial stuff? Did you talk with your child as you would a business associate or a stranger, in a matter-of-fact manner without any real emotion or closeness? Did you merely issue orders or commands, like a boss talking to an employee? Did you fall into a common trap for parents of giving only criticism or warnings? Did you feel like you and your child took a step forward in your relationship? Changing the way you communicate with your kids is not always easy. But in the long run, the payoff is worth the effort.

Take your kids on a "date." Whenever possible, pick a day and do something with your kids. Go to the park, ride bicycles, take a walk, go for a drive, or go window shopping. Go bowling, swimming, fishing, miniature golfing, boating, skating, to a movie, to the ice cream shop, or any place that's fun. This doesn't have to cost a lot of money, and your kids will love it. Doing fun things together is just another opportunity for parents and kids to enjoy each other's company.

Listen to your kids. Turn off the TV, put down the newspaper, look your child in the eyes, and really LISTEN to what he or she has to say.

Any time you turn down an invitation to listen to your child, you miss a great party. Your kids have a lot to say, and when you listen, it makes them feel worthwhile and important. That builds self-confidence and responsibility, two important traits for life.

Listening is a learned skill. You have to start doing it early with kids and continue to practice to stay good at it. Be patient and let your kids figure out what they want to say. Sometimes, you might not have to say a word. When your child is telling you a good story, just smile and nod. When your child is upset or wants to share how he or she handled a problem, simply reflect on what is said and reply with, "It sounds like that upset you" or "You handled that okay." Parents too often want to jump in and tell their kids what they should have done. Good listeners resist the urge to do that and wait for the child to ask for advice before offering help.

It's a busy world. You've got a lot on your mind and you may not always give top priority to what your children have to say. But if it's important enough for them to want to share it with you, it better go to the top of your list.

Tell your kids that you love them. Say "I love you" at least once a day. It can be in the morning when they leave for school or you leave for work or at night when they go to bed. Say it when you talk to them on the phone. Some folks may think this is corny. But a sincere expression of love never is.

As kids get older, they might get embarrassed when you say you love them in public (especially in front of their friends). Consider and understand their feelings. They still want you to say "I love you," just not when others are around.

Hug your kids. Young kids love this; older ones tolerate it; teens can't pull away fast enough. But even an arm around the shoulder and a quick squeeze is a wonderful expression of affection that, believe it or not, a child of any age appreciates.

Work with your kids. Anything you do with your kids – even work – is a relationship-building experience. Mow the lawn, rake leaves, clean the garage, do the dishes, cook a meal, clean house, go grocery shopping, or make something together. Doing chores or making repairs around the house together teaches kids that they are important members of the family and that everyone shares responsibility for taking care of the home. It's also a great way for kids to start learning how to do new tasks.

Play with your kids. Play a game, throw a football or a Frisbee®, do somersaults, dance, sing, run through the sprinklers, or just be silly. Too often, kids think that being with their parents is boring or a time for lectures or discipline. Lighten up. Life is supposed to be fun, and your kids are your joy. Laugh, smile, and show them that you know how to enjoy yourself.

Celebrate family traditions. A family's togetherness is often defined by how its members celebrate special events. Birthdays, anniversaries, and cultural, religious, or national holidays are exciting and important times for kids and adults. They are so important that memories of certain celebrations stay with people through their whole lives.

Most family traditions revolve around special events. For example, some families celebrate birthdays by going out to dinner at a restaurant chosen by the person having the birthday. For some families, a Fourth of July celebration isn't complete without a cookout and a fireworks display. Family gatherings are commonplace during holidays, and gift-giving is a part of many celebrations like Christmas and Hanukkah. Decorating the home or visiting relatives also are traditions that accompany special times of the year.

While most traditions are associated with holidays and other events, they also can be simple parts of daily life. Saying grace before meals, helping the younger kids set up a lemonade stand every summer, and baking cookies or making a meal for an elderly neighbor once a month are just a few examples of "small" but important traditions families can enjoy.

Traditions oftentimes are carried on from one generation to another. But it's easy for families to start new ones. Depending on your family's tastes and budget, traditions can range from something as simple as having a certain food for a holiday meal (turkey at Thanksgiving) to something as big as taking a vacation at the beach every summer. Whatever you choose, it will make being together as a family more fun and more memorable.

Have family meetings. For a family to function, it's important for everyone to know what's happening in the home and how decisions affect them. Family meetings are a great way for family members to share information with each other, plan schedules, solve problems, and discuss issues.

As a relationship-building opportunity, family meetings give kids an opportunity to offer their ideas and participate in the decision-making process. Obviously, there are some decisions that only parents can or should make. But allowing kids to have a voice in other matters, especially ones that directly affect them, is a good way to bring parents and kids closer together. Children see themselves as important members of the family and realize that what they think and feel counts. Parents who give kids this kind of responsibility are seen as caring and fair, and kids look forward to the family being together.

Family meetings are easy to do. First, decide how often you want to meet. Once every week or every two weeks is generally a good time frame. Next, put together some ground rules that everyone must follow. You might have a rule that says no one can embarrass a family member or use the meeting as a gripe session, or one that says family members have to take turns talking. Rules should be set up so meetings can run smoothly; family members also should decide on the consequences for breaking the rules. Also, choose a meeting time and a regular meeting place. (Popular times are after dinner on a weeknight or on Saturday mornings; popular meeting places are the kitchen or dining room table or the living room.)

Before a meeting, let everyone know when and where it will be. Put together an agenda of topics that

153

will be up for discussion. Everyone can help with this. When you get together, follow the agenda and let everyone express his or her opinions or ideas. Agenda items could include making a decision on where the family will go on vacation, changes in bedtimes for kids or chore schedules, information about upcoming school or sports events, or a discussion on whether to buy a new car.

Every family is busy. With work, school, and the million other activities that occur during the day, it seems like there's little time for getting together as a family. That's why it's so important to make time for family meetings. Just knowing that you will have an opportunity at least once a week to talk and "get reacquainted" can make a world of difference in relationships between parents and kids.

There is no substitute for the love you give your child or the time you spend with him or her. Nothing you do for or with your kids can be worthwhile unless a genuine bond of love exists. Building that strong, happy, healthy bond takes time and effort. It doesn't just happen. Pour yourself into your relationships with your children. Make every moment with them count.

CHAPTER 14

Catch Kids Being Good

You've just accomplished a goal at work, and you're feeling pretty good about it. You're even expecting some kind of recognition from the boss for a job well done. Days pass, and you don't hear a thing. Finally, frustrated, you give up hope of ever receiving any praise for your work.

Now think about how your child feels when he or she does something good and you either don't notice or fail to praise the accomplishment. Anger, frustration, sadness, and resentment are just a few of the negative emotions your child might feel. Worst of all, your child may not see any reason or have any motivation to repeat the positive behavior. He or she may figure, "What's the use? Nobody cares anyway." This is very hurtful and discouraging for children; everyone is quick to jump on their negative behaviors, but no one pays attention when they're good. This not only damages relationships but makes it difficult for parents to teach positive behaviors and convince children to use them.

Praising children is not always an easy thing to do. One problem is that our society tends to focus more attention on negatives than on positives. For example, a parent might punish his son and daughter by taking away TV every time they argue. But that parent might not praise the kids or reward them with extra TV time when they get along and play together. Another example is what is referred to in business as the "3:11" rule. This means that if you have a good meal in a restaurant, you're likely to tell three people about it. However, if you have a bad meal, you're likely to tell 11 people about it. Again, the negative overshadows the positive.

It's important to train yourself to notice and praise your kids' positive behaviors if you expect them to learn and continue to use those behaviors. The whole idea here is to recognize the good things your kids do so they will continue to do them. This is especially true when it comes to preventing or trying to reduce aggression or violence. Kids don't necessarily have to do something really special to merit praise, and parents can give it even when kids do what they are expected to do. Praise is such a powerful motivator for kids that it should be used all the time to recognize good behavior. Kids need to know when they've done something good or right, no matter how big or small the behavior is.

There are two kinds of praise. One is called "general praise." That means simply saying something like, "Great," "Good job," or "Way to go" when your child does something well. It's a quick way to let your child know that you noticed what he or she did and to offer encouragement. For example, you might use general praise when your child completes a daily chore like making his or her bed in the morning.

The second kind of praise is called **Effective Praise**. This easy-to-use method is especially helpful when you're praising your kids for:

- using a new behavior.
- improvements in behavior.
- positive attempts to learn new behaviors and skills.

Effective Praise is a great relationship-building tool. Nothing means more to your kids than your attention and approval of what they do. They love to please you, and when you tell them they have, they're happier and so are you. Yes, you still have to deal with negative behaviors, and that's not always a pleasant task. But consistently "catching 'em being good" helps kids grow as people who like themselves and are more self-confident.

157

There are four steps to Effective Praise. They are:

Step 1. Show your approval.

Be enthusiastic. Make your child feel good about what he or she did, and make him or her want to do it again. You can use words like, "Awesome," "Terrific," "Wow," "All right," "Wonderful," and "Fantastic." Throw in hugs, kisses, winks, smiles, a "thumbs up," a "high-five," clapping, or a pat on the back. Whatever words or actions you use, look at your child, be sincere, and let him or her know that you are happy about what happened.

Step 2. Describe the positive behavior.

Specifically describe what you saw or heard so your child knows exactly what the praise is for and what behavior you want to see him or her repeat. Use words your kids understand, and be brief and to the point. For example, say "Thanks for taking care of your brother while I was gone. It makes me happy to know that I can depend on you like that."

Step 3. Give a reason for using the behavior.

As we've said before, giving a reason helps kids understand the connection between what they do and what happens to them or others. Reasons are especially important in Effective Praise because they usually spell out the benefits kids will receive as a result of a positive behavior. This encourages kids to use the behavior in the future. Reasons should be brief, appropriate for the child's age, and believable. For example, don't tell a 7-year-old that sharing his toys with a friend is important because it shows maturity. A 7-year-old won't get it. Instead, say "If you share your toys with your friends, your friends will probably share their toys with you."

Step 4. Give a reward (optional).

Occasionally, you may want to reward your child for a certain behavior, a big improvement, or for doing something special. Rewards can be big or small, but the size should fit the behavior you're trying to encourage.

One key to success is remembering to praise a positive behavior immediately after it occurs. This makes the connection between positive behaviors and praise stronger. Kids start thinking: "When I shared my toys, Mom noticed and told me I did a good job. I like that." If you're already using Effective Praise and aren't seeing any results, look at whether you're not praising enough, praising too much (not making your praise dependent on positive behavior), or praising the wrong behaviors.

What's Ahead?

A few years ago, a movie called *Problem Child* hit the theaters. The film was about a mischievous 7-year-old boy who is adopted by a couple eager to have a child. The day the boy moves into his new home, he sets fire to his room and causes such a ruckus that his adoptive grandfather has to be taken to the hospital. As the movie goes on, the boy's antics become even more outrageous: "Junior" puts firecrackers in a birthday cake, sticks a vacuum hose in the goldfish bowl, and fills the cat's water dish with detergent. In one scene, he looks at a nun and says to himself, "I wonder if penguins can fly." A few minutes later, the nun is dangling from a rope outside an upper-story window. Through all of this, Junior's adoptive parents shower him with love and affection as they struggle to live with and understand his aggressive, often destructive behavior. (It turns out that Junior has been in and out of 30 adoptive homes because no one can handle him.)

The movie is a comedy, so all of Junior's escapades are played for laughs and no one is seriously hurt. Junior and his adoptive parents are Hollywood's version of the typical American family, and the characters and situations are so silly and unrealistic that the whole story borders on the ridiculous. But though it tries to be humorous, the movie disturbingly depicts a situation that happens far too often in real life: Parents have a child who uses aggression to get what he or she wants or to settle differences. They love their child and want to help change his or her behaviors, but they don't know how. So the child's misbehaviors continue and perhaps worsen, the parents become frustrated by their inability to "fix" the problem, and family relationships are strained and damaged.

Boys Town's mission is to help children and parents who face this dilemma. We start with this message for parents: Don't give up on your kids. Don't give up hope for change. It can happen with the right plan and the right tools. That's what this book offers. The teaching methods and relationship-building suggestions we've discussed here are the starting points for a new way to reach your children. They are practical, easy-to-use, and most importantly, effective.

Boys Town knows these methods work because thousands of parents have successfully used them to help their kids change their behaviors for the better.

We don't claim to have all the answers; when it comes to working with aggressive children, there are no guarantees or "miracle cures." Every family's problems are different, and preventing or reducing aggression takes time and a lot of effort. Parents and children have to learn to trust each other and work together. And changing your children's behavior might mean changing your own behavior. Those are huge tasks. How well you adapt what's in this book to your situation and your parenting style will determine how successful you will be.

In some cases, children may need more help than parents can provide. For a child whose behaviors have become so serious or violent that they pose a danger to the child or others, counseling, therapy, and other interventions by professionals may be necessary. Parents must be willing to accept these situations and find appropriate help. This isn't an easy decision, but loving parents understand that tough decisions have to be made sometimes for the good of their child.

Your children are our future. What they learn from you now will affect them for the rest of their lives. We have confidence in your abilities as a good parent. We know you love and care about your kids.

We know you want what's best for them. Give yourself a pat on the back for trying to make the future brighter and happier for your family and your kids.

Boys Town has several other excellent resources for information on parenting and child-care issues.

- The toll-free Boys Town National Hotline (1-800-448-3000) takes calls 24 hours a day, 7 days a week to provide guidance and information for children and parents with problems.

- *Common Sense Parenting®* (2nd edition) is an award-winning book that received an "outstanding" rating from The Parent Council®. The book and other parenting resources are available through the Boys Town Press, 1-800-282-6657.

- For details on parenting classes that Boys Town offers across the country, call 1-402-498-1072, or contact Boys Town's Internet website at www.ffbh.boystown.org.

Index

V

W

Book Credits

Editing: Ron Herron
Content Specialist: Tom Dowd
Production: Mary Steiner
Cover Design: Margie Brabec
Page Layout: Anne Hughes